B 25

TAROT

A T MANN has practised astrology and tarot professionally for more than 20 years, and has written many books on these and other subjects. His books include *Life Time Astrology*, *Sacred Sexuality* and *Sacred Architecture*.

D0041369

New Perspectives

THE SERIES

New Perspectives provide attractive and accessible introductions to a comprehensive range of mind, body and spirit topics. Beautifully designed and illustrated, these practical books are written by experts in each subject.

Titles in the series include:

ALEXANDER TECHNIQUE
by Richard Brennan

MASSAGE
by Stewart Mitchell

AROMATHERAPY
by Christine Wildwood

MEDITATION
by David Fontana

DREAMS
by David Fontana

NLP
by Carol Harris

FENG SHUI
by Man-Ho Kwok with Joanne O'Brien

NUMEROLOGY
by Rodford Barrat

FLOWER REMEDIES
by Christine Wildwood

REFLEXOLOGY
by Inge Dougans

HOMEOPATHY
by Peter Adams

TAROT
by A T Mann

New Perspectives

TAROT

An Introductory Guide to Unlocking the Secrets of the Tarot

A T MANN

ELEMENT

Shaftesbury, Dorset • Boston, Massachusetts
Melbourne, Victoria

First published as *The Elements of Tarot*
in 1993 by Element Books Limited

This revised edition first published in Great Britain
in 1999 by Element Books Limited, Shaftesbury, Dorset SP7 8BP

Published in the USA in 1999 by Element Books, Inc.
160 North Washington Street,
Boston, MA 02114

Published in Australia in 1999 by
Element Books and distributed by
Penguin Australia Limited
487 Maroondah Highway,
Ringwood, Victoria 3134

Designed for Element Books Limited by
Design Revolution, Queens Park Villa,
30 West Drive, Brighton, East Sussex BN2 2GE

ELEMENT BOOKS LIMITED
Editorial Director: Sarah Sutton
Editorial Manager: Jane Pizzey
Commissioning Editor: Grace Cheetham
Production Director: Roger Lane

DESIGN REVOLUTION
Editorial Director: Ian Whitelaw
Art Director: Lindsey Johns
Editor: Julie Whitaker
Designer: Vanessa Good

Printed and bound in Great Britain by
Bemrose Security Printing, Derby

British Library Cataloguing in Publication
data available

Library of Congress Cataloging in Publication
data available

ISBN 1-86204-673-5

Contents

Acknowledgements

I would like to thank my friend and associate Derek Seagrief for reading parts of the text and for his penetrating and perceptive comments. I thank Michael Mann for suggesting the book and Julia McCutchen for her help in editing the text. And I thank my wife Lise-Lotte for her helpful comments and support throughout the process of writing this book.

WHAT IS THE TAROT?

CHAPTER ONE

Tarot is one of the most important forms of Western mysticism. The symbolism of the cards has stimulated and attracted truth seekers for over 600 years. Historically, the tarot is seen as a mantic art, a form of divination, a way of knowing about the future. However, the traditions from which the tarot emerged, and the interest it has aroused in aware and enlightened people, signal its higher functions. The proper use and understanding of the ancient and mystical art of the tarot cards can lead to a recognition of the existence of hidden knowledge within the psyche, awakening deeper layers of soul experience.

The tarot cards are symbolic keys whose function is to open up the psyche to new ideas, concepts, feelings and spiritual possibilities. Tarot symbols both conceal and reveal their mysteries according to our ability to concentrate or meditate upon them. The deeper we can go into their world, the more they will awaken true contact with the soul.

The tarot is a system with many sources – astrology, cabbala, numer-ology, alchemy, magic, mythology, Christian mysticism, Egyptology, religion, Eastern philosophy, psychology and metaphysic – yet its form makes it available to everyone, whatever their level of understanding. In this sense, it is unique.

HOW DOES THE TAROT FUNCTION?

The oldest beliefs about the tarot can be described by the term *cartomancy*, that is, divination by cards. It was believed that mysterious Fate guides the shuffling and selection of cards. Each moment has a unique and magical quality that is divined by, and reflected in, the cards, just as it may also be seen by reading tea leaves, clouds in the sky, bones, the entrails of animals, stones, seeds or dice. The random shuffling of the pack mixes the vocabulary of symbols contained within the cards into a chaotic jumble, and the act of laying the cards out creates order from that primal chaos. At any moment, the cards that are drawn reflect the qualities of the time, just as the seemingly irrelevant images of a dream may be seen to identify particular issues emerging from the unconscious self.

If the cards and their actions are the outer form of the mystery of tarot, the inner secret is about how and why they have such a profound effect upon us.

Their operation in the realm of the psyche is becoming more important although the use of tarot for divination is not diminishing in favour of its use as a tool for personal transformation.

Tarot demonstrates that the inner psyche not only has a profound relationship with outer events, but also provides a symbolic mirror for them. The tarot reading produces certain combinations of symbols that reflect the state of the psyche of the querent (the one who asks the questions) at a given moment, and provides the inner and outer guidance required to understand a current situation, or for initiating the next stage of the process.

This seems an absurd idea, but in recent decades it is a concept that has gained acceptance in the domain of physics and psychology. The objective external viewpoint valued by modern science has been proven to be a fantasy, a logical impossibility. Physicists have realized, despite their initial resistance, that the mere fact that they observe events in the physical world has an effect upon those events. This implies that it is essential to recognize the influence of an observer on the experiment, or that being conscious and present has an effect on the outcome of your life. The truth of this concept has been proven in experiments in the micro-world of particle physics, where the illumination and measurement of subatomic collisions affect the outcome of the experiment. If the experiment were unobserved, it would not occur in the same way. This is also true in life. Learning to observe yourself experiencing your life will affect you in profound ways.

Thus the subjective state of a querent has an effect upon the results of the shuffling and layout of the cards, just as in modern physics the expectations of the physicist are known to have an effect upon the results of the experiment. Our state of mind is a primary factor in our present and future unfolding.

Tarot is an ideal process through which to observe, interpret and interact with the operations of the psyche. The images of the cards only reflect what is happening inside, and the way you understand these images parallels the way in which you understand and act in your life. Tarot is a near-perfect mirror of your being.

9

LEFT THE LAYOUT OF THE CARDS IS LARGELY DETERMINED BY THE PSYCHOLOGICAL STATE OF THE QUERENT AND REFLECTS WHAT IS HAPPENING WITHIN HIM OR HER.

THE MAGICIAN

ORIGINS AND HISTORY
OF THE TAROT

Tarot decks are unique because they have 22 picture cards known as Major Arcana, used together with a Minor Arcana of 56 cards, which are similar to traditional playing cards, plus the addition of four extra face cards, making a deck of 78 cards. The word *arcana* means 'secret' or 'mysterious' in Latin.

The first tarot decks appeared in Europe in the 15th century. The exact date or origin of the cards is unknown, and there are many candidates for the first Tarot deck. They may have been influenced by pictorial cards brought back from the East by the crusading Knights Templar during the late 13th century, but no-one knows for sure.

Many derivations have been suggested for the name tarot. It may come from the Latin word *rota* (wheel), which is an anagram of taro and was a magical formula utilized by the Brotherhood of the Rosy Cross (it is used in some decks on the Wheel of Fortune card). The Egyptian word *ta-rosh* means 'the royal way,' and it has been suggested that tarot is derived from the name of the Egyptian god of writing and magic, Thoth. Others, who accept its Hebrew origin, see tarot as a corruption of the *Torah*, the Book of the Law. On the most exoteric level, *tar* is the gypsy word for a deck of cards.

The earliest tarots are decorated with medieval images and symbols, and have names such as the Pope, Emperor, Empress, High

ABOVE THE HANGED MAN
FROM THE 15TH-CENTURY
VISCONTI-SFORZA TAROT.
THIS CARD IS DECORATED
WITH GOLD LEAF AND HAS
A LUXURIOUS FINISH.

Priestess, Fool, Magician and Hanged Man, all members of medieval society. The early decks were individually hand-painted, while later decks were block-printed and hand coloured until the popularization of the printing press centuries later.

The Visconti-Sforza tarocchi cards are one of the earliest known decks, painted in the mid-1400s for the Duke of Milan. The surviving cards of the deck are now in museum collections in New York and Italy. This deck was hand-painted as a wedding present for a union between the Visconti and Sforza families. Francois Fibbia, the Prince of Pisa in exile, invented a deck of tarot cards very similar to those known today, composed of 40 numbered cards and 22 arcana cards. As Fibbia died in 1415, his deck is among the very earliest.

11

The 15th-century Mantegna deck is a beautiful and unusual deck of tarot cards, numbered from 1 to 50, divided into 5 classes of 10 cards each. The deck is an image of the universal order as perceived at the time, and portrays a sequence of evolutionary stages from the Prima Causa (Creation) to the Beggar (corresponding to the Fool in modern decks). In Series A are the spheres of creation and the sun, moon and planets; Series B and C contain 13 of the liberal arts such as grammar, geometry, philosophy, astrology, theology and cosmology; Series D contains Apollo and the nine muses; while Series E is similar to traditional tarot in including images of the pope, the emperor, the king, the doge, the knight, gentleman, a merchant, artisan, valet and beggar. These cards are now in the British Museum.

ABOVE THE MANTEGNA DECK
CAN BE USED AS EITHER A
GAME OR A SET OF MORAL
AND PHILOSOPHICAL LESSONS.

The Marseilles deck appeared towards the end of the 15th century, using similar subjects but different designs, and retaining the use of the four suits. In the Marseilles deck, the Fool is unnumbered and the other major arcana cards have roman numerals. This deck has remained one of the most colourful and popular ever since.

ABOVE THE LOVERS CARD FROM THE MARSEILLES TAROT. THIS FRENCH DECK, DATED TO THE 15TH CENTURY, WAS PROBABLY THE EARLIEST STANDARDIZED TAROT DECK.

Many believe that tarot cards are of much more ancient origin than the earliest decks. The 18th-century scholar, Court de Gébelin (1725–84), claimed that the Major Arcana were symbolic of the stages of the Egyptian or Chaldean mysteries. He proposed that the 22 Major Arcana cards were remnants of the *Book of Thoth*, who was the Egyptian god of writing. He believed that tarot described the creation of the world. The designs that accompanied his book, *Le Monde Primitif* (*The Primitive World*), which was published in 1781, are the foundation upon which later traditional decks were designed.

19th-century philosopher and cabbalist Eliphas Lévi identified the source of tarot wisdom and symbolism as the sacred Enochian alphabet of the Hebrews, which had previously been recorded on tablets of gold and ivory, decorated with precious stones and gilt. The Hebrew alphabet has 22 letters, the same number as the Major Arcana, and its associated Tree of Life has 22 paths between the 10 Sephiroth. Lévi believed that, even when the tarot did not predict, it revealed something hidden to the wise.

A French scholar Gerard Encausse (1865–1917), whose magical name in the Rosicrucian and masonic orders was Papus, believed that the entire wisdom transmitted in the tarot was central to the Egyptian mystery religion and that its function was as an initiation device. Encausse also introduced Hebrew number symbolism, which is known as *gematria*, into the tarot in the numbering and numerical value of the cards.

However, it was Dr Arthur Edward Waite (1857–1942), a member of the mystical Order of the Golden Dawn, who transformed the use of the tarot in modern times. Waite explored the symbolism of the tarot in his book, *The Key to the Tarot.*

He also designed a deck that was painted by the artist Pamela Coleman Smith, known as the Rider-Waite deck. Waite developed the magical and symbolic aspects of the Major Arcana cards, introducing many Hermetic and Rosicrucian images. He also created for the first time images for the 10 numbered cards of the four suits. Previously, all decks had simply portrayed the numbered cards in a similar manner to playing card pips. For example, the eight of swords had been a design of eight swords on a card. Waite's deck, however, shows this card as a young woman tied up and blindfolded, surrounded by eight swords plunged into the ground, in front of a hill town fortress.

ABOVE WAITE'S DECK WAS THE FIRST TO DEPICT SYMBOLIC SCENES ON THE MINOR ARCANA CARDS, AS IN THIS EIGHT OF SWORDS. HE ALSO GAVE DIVINATORY MEANINGS TO THESE CARDS.

13

Aleister Crowley, one of the most controversial magicians of the 20th century, designed the Thoth deck with the artist Lady Freida Harris in the 1940s. It is perhaps the most symbolic and colourful deck ever produced. His deck contains Egyptian, Eastern, Greek, medieval and Christian symbolism, and in

14

its structure synthesized the traditions of numerology, alchemy, cabbala and astrology. Crowley saw the tarot as a magical encyclopedia and as a key to the mysteries that could be utilized by a magician in order to invoke their various energies. The tarot cards were to him a form of archetypal intelligence that could be incorporated within the psyche.

In recent years the tarot has become extremely popular and there are now many different contemporary decks. Decks have been made using as their foundation the symbolic systems of women, the Earth Mother goddesses, Native Americans, Celts, Arthurian knights, and a myriad of others.

Some of these are worthy of exploration, but many of the newer decks have strayed away from the central concept of the tarot and its archetypal language.

THE MAGICIAN

STRUCTURE
AND SYMBOLISM
OF THE TAROT

CHAPTER THREE

The tarot contains elements of many representative Western mystery traditions. Indeed, it is astonishing how many different philosophical, religious, psychological and magical systems it seems able to reflect. Successive commentators state that the tarot has one particular true meaning, and all the others are secondary, and that the many cultures now represented in tarot decks all derive from the same archetypal foundations.

The adaptability of the tarot is characteristic of a system that arises from the archetypal domain. The cards are powerful because they are images upon which a viewer can project aspects of the self. We can easily see the Fool, the Eternal Child, the Wise Old Man, the Emperor, the Empress, the Pope, the Hanged Man and Death as archetypal images that exist in us all at some deeper level of development. The tarot is, therefore, a supreme tool for learning to communi-cate with the archetypes of the collective unconscious.

DEATH.

ABOVE THE TAROT CARDS DEPICT ARCHETYPAL IMAGES. BY WORKING WITH THE CARDS, WE CAN MAKE CONTACT WITH THE ARCHETYPES THAT EXIST WITHIN US ON AN UNCONSCIOUS LEVEL.

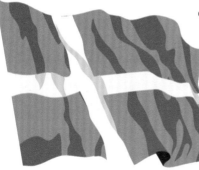

The tarot also utilizes a vocabulary of symbols to carry its meaning. A symbol is the manifestation of an archetypal pattern that has multiple meanings.

Thus, a cross may mean Christianity, the Earth, a hospital or the national flag of Denmark, according to the orientation and background of the observer. Symbols activate instinctive parts of us that may have lain dormant for years or lifetimes, and often carry many layers of meaning simultaneously.

ABOVE SYMBOLS SUCH AS THE CROSS CARRY A MYRIAD OF MEANINGS AND USUALLY REPRESENT SOMETHING MUCH MORE PROFOUND THAT THE OBJECT ITSELF.

16

At the most basic level, tarot is a universal structure expressing a vocabulary of archetypal symbols. Understanding the structure and the symbols and their meaning will allow one to decode any tarot deck, and indeed any archetypal images found in our lives.

COMMON TAROT SYMBOLS

In order to use the cards it is important to understand some of the more common symbols. These symbols are archetypal in that they activate contents within our memories or collective unconscious that are not always available to our conscious minds.

Pairs of columns appear in a number of the cards (High Priestess, the Hierophant and Justice). They symbolize the physical world and its vested authorities. The Greek Iamblichus was initiated into the Egyptian mysteries and saw a temple with 22 pairs of columns, between each of which were frescos depicting mystical figures and symbols. Each picture represented a stage of the initiation process and is reproduced in the tarot cards. The columns in some of the cards may be symbolic of this mystery temple. Such column pairs are also gateways from one place to another, but, more importantly, from one state of mind or attitude to another. These cards, therefore, symbolize transition and permanent change of values. When there are black and white columns, such as in the High Priestess, they also show dualities such as male/female, conscious/unconscious, right/left, etc. Where the columns are abstracted, such as in the card of the Chariot, they signify taking on authority oneself.

Stars and canopies symbolize the higher world that is available through increased awareness. Stars symbolize the astrological qualities that synchronize with our life pattern, and show the higher language of the heavens. They often represent actual zodiac constellations or constellations such as the Pleiades or Sirius, which were worshipped by the Egyptians and other cultures. The stars are also bodies encasing the spirit, mind and soul. In esoteric astrology, the seven stars of the Great Bear represent the seven solar systems from which the present world evolved.

17

The **throne** is dominion, power, strength and fixed being, often associated with royalty. In some of the cards the throne is symbolic of the domain of the archetype, for example, in the Empress where the throne is created in nature and indeed is the natural world, or in the Devil, where the throne is a black cube of stone to which the female and male natures are chained. Both the throne and cube are symbolic of the physical world itself.

The **pyramid** is the resolution and transfiguration of the physical world symbolized by the four sides at its base and the higher, transcendent reality symbolized by the apex or crown.

The **square** and the **triangle** are the plane symbols of the cube and pyramind in two dimensions. The square is the physical world, solidity and persistence, and signifies the human being who is not evolved and who has not achieved inner unity. The triangle is the trinity, the resolution of duality by a third, higher integrating influence at its apex, which is often taken to be consciousness. When

•

the triangle points downwards it shows immersion in matter, dominance by the body or physical demands and, finally, the principle of unconsciousness.

The **sphere** symbolizes god, completion and also the cosmos within which all activity takes place. When it is surmounted by a cross, it is the orb of worldly power with spiritual understanding or papal dominance.

Towers symbolize the act of rising above the mundane physical world to higher realms, a means of ascent, and a linking of earth to heaven. The windows shown in a tower may indicate the various levels of being within the human body, with the higher windows representing higher qualities. A lighthouse is high illumination. Twin towers show the duality between individual power and life energy.

The **crown** is dominion, royal position and high status. Many believe it to be a physical reflection of the human aura that demonstrates our level of spiritual development in its colours. The triple tiara shows power over the three worlds of the physical, emotional and mental domains.

The **sceptre** is a magic wand. It is symbolic of the thunderbolt or the phallus as a source of energy and fertility. It is also linked to the world axis. The sceptre is also often abstracted as the fleur-de-lys, which is fairly commonly found in decorations on the tarot cards.

ABOVE A CROWN SYMBOLIZES SOVEREIGNTY AND LOFTY STATUS. IT IS ALSO BELIEVED TO BE A PHYSICAL REPRESENTATION OF THE HUMAN AURA, WHICH REVEALS OUR LEVEL OF SPIRITUAL DEVELOPMENT.

Keys open the secret doctrine, to unlock the recesses of ourselves.

An **arrow** is the will, spirit or the energy and one-pointedness of the element fire.

A **snake** symbolizes time, and when forming a circle biting its tail or in the figure of eight shape (also known as the lemniscate) is infinity. It signifies the cyclic nature of the world and energy required to power the cycles of life.

Corn is fertility and plenty as a symbol of the Great Mother or grain goddess, as well as of ritual fertilization, death and renewal. The **cornfield** is fertility and a loving environment.

Roses are symbols of love, but also mystical and alchemical correlates with the heart.

Trees are the process of evolution and integration. In ancient times they were sacred spirits and the way by which spirits descended to the world and by which the souls of humanity reached heaven.

ABOVE SNAKES ARE A COMMON SYMBOL IN THE TAROT (ON THE MAGICIAN'S BELT FOR EXAMPLE). THEY OFTEN SYMBOLIZE INFINITY.

Because the **sunflower** moves with the sun, it is solar and leonine.

The **dog** is loyalty, instinct and faithfulness, as well as being the guardian of the underworld of the unconscious. **Cats** are the perceptive power and pure consciousness of the feminine.

ABOVE DOGS ARE A SYMBOL OF FIDELITY AND PROTECTIVENESS. THEY ARE ALSO TRADITIONAL GUARDIANS OF THE UNDERWORLD OF THE UNCONSCIOUS.

Eagles and **hawks** are temporal power, dominion and strength. They fly with the sun god and, when symbolized with a solar disc, are Egyptian deities.

The **phoenix** is a symbol of rebirth and renewal through destruction.

THE SYMBOLIC MEANINGS OF NUMBERS

The primary structural device in tarot is number. Each Major Arcana card not only has a numerical value but also a Roman numeral that places it in sequence. The numbers and numerals describe their relationship with each other and the whole.

Each suit of the Minor arcana is numbered from the ace to 10. Each card carries its quality as a number in addition to its other symbolism, and also its significance as a particular stage of a process.

Zero is non-being, the opposite of unity, the latent potential of creativity, the non-manifest and the state of death during which life is transformed. Zero can be symbolized by blackness, empty space, the underworld and the world egg enwrapped by a snake.

ABOVE THE NUMBER ONE CAN BE SYMBOLIZED BY THE HEBREW LETTER *ALEPH.*

One is the point, the centre, the focus of creativity, pure spirit, unity and the reduction of all other numbers (all numbers can be divided by one). It can be symbolized by a point or a circle or a sphere, a single centralized object or the Hebrew letter *aleph.*

Two is the line, duality, the periphery, an echo, reflection, the shadow and represents the quality of the attraction of opposites that is contained in all processes. It is symbolized by the full or new moon, heaven and earth, black and white squares, pairs of columns, shadows, twins, the yin/yang.

Three is the plane, balance and resolution, synthesis and creation, heaven, the action of unity upon duality. It is symbolized by the triangle, the three dimensions, the trinity.

Four is the solid, manifest world, earth, the physical domain and the quaternity of integration as the four elements or the four psychological types. It is symbolized by the cross, square and cube, the four cardinal points, four fixed zodiac signs and the beasts of the Biblical Apocalypse or Ezekiel.

ABOVE THE STAR , WITH ITS FIVE POINTS, IS A COMMON SYMBOL FOR THE NUMBER FIVE.

Five is human, time, the quintessence of being, the centre of the manifest universe. It is symbolized by the pentagram and pentagon, and the square or cube with a central point, the star, the human body, the golden section mathematical proportion derived from the pentagon that governs the pattern of growth in some plants.

Six is equilibrium, the human soul, self consciousness capable of experience, the six directions of space, trial and effort. It is symbolized by the Seal of Solomon or the Star of David, an upward and downward pointing triangle of the elements intersecting, and the elemental plane.

Seven is perfect order, bliss, the essence of being, the completion of a cycle or period, the chakras, the planetary spheres and their gods and goddesses. It is symbolized by the seven planets, the constellation of the Great Bear, the rainbow colours, the chakra lotuses, the musical scale, and the Seal of Solomon with a point of spirit in the centre.

21

RIGHT SEVEN IS THE NUMBER OF THE RAINBOW, THERE BEING SEVEN COLOURS IN ITS MANIFESTATION.

Eight is thought and intellection, the doubled quaternity, the resurrection, the enclosure, the eight cardinal and intermediate directions, the firmament or realm of the fixed stars. It is symbolized by the eight-pointed star, the double square or double cube, the caduceus and the infinity symbol.

Nine is the tripled trinity, being, pleasure, truth, the mystic number, integration of physical, intellectual and spiritual worlds. It is symbolized by three intersecting triangles.

Ten is the return to unity, spiritual achievement, the totality of the universe, and perfection. Ten can be symbolized by two intersecting pentacles.

Eleven is transition, excess and conflict, duality that is incapable of resolution.

Twelve is cosmic order and salvation, the astrological language, the year, the wheel of becoming. It is symbolized by the zodiac or rings of flowers.

LEFT THESE TWO INTERSECTING PENTANGLES ARE SOMETIMES USED TO SYMBOLIZE THE NUMBER TEN.

Butterflies and **bees** are symbolic of the soul, rebirth and eternal life.

Crabs, **lobsters** and other crustaceans emerge, like humanity, from the unconscious sea and represent the fertilizing power of water.

Mountains symbolize the quest, the need to ascend, meditation and higher realms of the self. Mountains in the distance imply the embarkation upon the journey to wholeness.

Lightning is inspiration and a direct communication with the gods and goddesses, intuition and divine intercession.

Barren landscapes are devoid of love and affection.

ASTROLOGY AND THE CARDS

The connections between the Major Arcana and the elements, astrological signs and planets form a primary structure of the tarot.

The correlation is particularly valuable because astrology defines very clear personality types, and assigns physical and psychological actions to individual signs, planets and aspects between planets, all of which can be used to enrich further the tarot symbolism.

ABOVE THE LION IS A SYMBOL OF BOTH THE TAROT (THE STRENGTH CARD) AND ASTROLOGY (THE SIGN LEO). THERE ARE MANY OTHER SYMBOLS COMMON TO BOTH DIVINATORY SYSTEMS.

Astrological symbols can be commonly found in the tarot. The lion in the Strength card obviously correlates with the sign Leo; the Chariot, with lunar crescents outside the walls of a city, evokes the sign Cancer; similarly the lunar images of the High Priestess mark her as a goddess of the moon; the garden couch of the Empress is decorated with a Venus symbol upon a heart, clearly evoking the goddess of love; the Tower is destroyed by a burst of energy, which is obviously of the planet Mars; and the Sun card literally corresponds to the astrological symbolism of the sun.

ABOVE TAROT AND ASTROLOGY ARE COMPLEMENTARY SYSTEMS OF DIVINATION AND MANY EXPONENTS OF THE TAROT LINK THE CARDS TO THE PLANETS.

THE MAGICIAN

r THE MAJOR
ARCANA CARDS

CHAPTER FOUR

The 22 Major Arcana cards describe the process from the pure state of the unnumbered Fool to the completion of the World. Each card will be described, to draw attention to the images, symbols and their interaction in the overall composition of the card. The symbolic interpretation of the card identifies the inner, psychological meaning of the images and actions portrayed in the card, as well as an initiatory lesson to be learned from the card. The guided imagery helps to provide the atmosphere of discovery and inner experience associated with the card (*see* also Creative Visualization, p.118). The section on meaning describes the manifestations of the card and its symbolism in life situations, often called the divinatory meaning of the cards.

ABOVE THERE ARE 22 MAJOR ARCANA CARDS IN A TAROT DECK. NUMBERED FROM ZERO (THE FOOL) TO 21 (THE WORLD), THE CARDS CAN BE SEEN AS A SYMBOLIC JOURNEY THROUGH LIFE.

Many tarot books also give meanings for a reversed card. These often describe negative qualities associated with the cards. Occasionally the negative meanings bear little relationship to the upright significance of the cards. For example, Arthur Waite describes the divinatory meaning of the Magician reversed as 'Physician, Magus, mental disease, disgrace, disquiet'. However, it is no longer standard Tarot practice to designate reversed meanings for the cards. In reality, the reversed cards signify shadow qualities, the underlying unconscious motives that are other, sometimes darker, aspects of our being that are as yet inseparable from our totality. These shadow qualities simply bring the lighter qualities into sharper focus. The reversed card also signifies the need for the querent to penetrate more deeply into the hidden significance of a certain time or quality.

The affirmation is a useful device for coming into a deeper and more immediate relationship with the qualities embodied in the cards (*see* also Affirmations, p.119).

THE FOOL

THE SPIRIT OF AETHYR

ARCANUM ZERO

THE PLANET URANUS AND THE ELEMENT AIR

KEY WORD: INDIVIDUATION

A questing and confident youth begins his journey standing on a mountain precipice high above the world. He looks up rather than down, despite the dog barking at his heels. He wears beautiful clothes decorated with mystical symbols and a fool's cap with a feather. Suspended from the wand over his shoulder is an embroidered bag containing his worldly possessions. He holds a rose in his left hand and his face is intelligent, blissful and radiant, like the sun at his back. He is the pure man, awaiting the experiences of the world that will fulfil his expectations and dreams.

THE SYMBOLIC FOOL

The Fool is the eternal child beginning the journey to enlightenment, symbolized by his ambiguous number zero and his daring descent from the top of the mountain. He is the element Air representing the spontaneous mind that contains our fantasies, projections, thoughts and understanding, but which is uncontrolled and prone to erratic and unpredictable behaviour, characteristic of the planet Uranus. His zodiacal belt symbolizes his journey to individuation through the planetary spheres. He carries all the elements except the sword of discrimination (*see* p.69) – he believes too readily and can easily be misled by outer appearances or attractive ideas. He is an empty canvas waiting for a painter who can take risks.

GUIDED IMAGERY

'Having effortlessly ascended to the mountain top, you survey the beautiful landscape below the mountain peak upon which you stand. Your shadow, cast by the powerful sun at your back, extends across hill and vale, integrating itself within the marvellous and beautiful landscape below, breaking down into thousands of details, and changing its overall form from moment to moment. As you spontaneously leap across the first precipice towards an unknown destiny in the far distance, you realize that

LEFT THE FOOL IS THE CHILD WITHIN US, IMPULSIVE AND RECKLESS. LIKE A CHILD, HE IS ENTHUSIASTIC AND BEGINS LIFE'S ADVENTURES WITH DISREGARD FOR THE CONSEQUENCES.

you must descend through that shadow that moves as you do, beyond into the clear light of day.'

THE MEANING

Childlike enthusiasm; awakening perceptions of the world; mental spontaneity leading either to folly or wisdom. Beginning an adventure without considering the consequences carefully. An 'all or none' attitude.

AFFIRMATION

'The truth and radiance of my inner child will guide me through unlimited possibilities as I venture out into the unknown world.'

THE MAGICIAN

THE MAGUS OF POWER

ARCANUM ONE
THE PLANET MERCURY
KEY WORD: INITIATION

THE MAGICIAN.

A magically robed youth holds a wand aloft in his right hand, while pointing down to the flower-covered ground with his left, linking the spiritual with the earthly world. He looks down upon the pentacle, cup, sword and wand, his magical implements, on the table. Floating above his head is the horizontal figure-of-eight, the lemniscate or infinity sign, showing the attainment of eternal knowledge in life. The columns supporting the table indicate the need to raise consciousness above the world of the senses. The red and white motif of flowers and his robes show that he embodies the synthesis of physical and spiritual worlds.

THE SYMBOLIC MAGICIAN

The magician is the mind, alternately instinctive and profound, which must be juggled and empowered by our will. He is concentrated without effort, and guided by inner rhythms. The magic of Mercury brings down higher virtue to things below and allows communication between levels within. The pentacle, cup, sword and wand are his magical implements that symbolize the divine in the four elements expressed through the psychological types – the aspects of the self that must be brought into balance. They lie upon the four-fold table, which is the firmament and foundation of the human endeavour towards synthesis.

ABOVE THE HORIZONTAL FIGURE-OF-EIGHT THAT APPEARS ABOVE THE HEAD OF THE MAGICIAN DENOTES INFINITY AND THE ATTAINMENT OF ETERNAL KNOWLEDGE.

28

The double-ended wand, the red and white colours, and his upward and downward pointing gestures all illustrate the duality that the magician within us must conquer with wisdom. The infinity symbol over his head and the snake biting its tail around his waist imply that the ability to find unity through meditation and concentration lies above and around us.

GUIDED IMAGERY

'As you walk within the walled garden on a radiant day, a stream symbolizing life energy parts it in two. The bridge joining the halves is the higher mind, and the power of the magician within you depends upon knowing both sides. As you cross over, you become aware of the elevated view the bridge affords, making you feel bright and confident of inner ideas. The darkness and insecurity in the recesses of your changeable mind become transformed into the light of conscious wisdom within the self. The transformation happens in a divine instant, bringing together your contradictory parts. You are juggling the pentacle, cup, wand and sword in a masterly way, knowing that they are the tools of your enlightenment. Now you see the light is within yourself.'

THE MEANING

Exploration of consciousness leads to wisdom; the search for meaning as a magical action; transforming the basic material of the unaware self. The correct application of willpower depends upon adapting to existing forces, preferring thought over action. Communication skills bring access to the divine.

AFFIRMATION

'I will concentrate without effort, pay attention, and transform work into play, thereby communicating magical talents through my clarity of self.'

THE HIGH PRIESTESS

PRIESTESS OF THE SILVER STAR

ARCANUM TWO
THE MOON
KEY WORD: HIDDEN KNOWLEDGE

THE HIGH PRIESTESS

The High Priestess in early tarot decks is called the Papess, evoking the mythical Pope Joan of the ninth century. She is also Juno, the priestess Diana of the Eleusinian mysteries or the Celtic triple goddess. The High Priestess contains the many dimensions of feminine power, expressing the polarity between masculine law and feminine imagination. Standing on a waxing crescent moon, she wears the blue vestments and crown (the two horn-shaped crescents astride a lunar orb) of the

Egyptian goddess, Isis. On her chest is a solar cross and under her robes she carries the scrolls of the Hebrew *Torah* (with the last letter hidden), because in her antiquity she contains pagan, Egyptian, Jewish and Christian authority. Her cubic throne of unadorned and pure matter sits between black and white lotus pillars of the Egyptian mystery temple.

THE SYMBOLIC HIGH PRIESTESS

Indigo and silver colours, the horns and orb of Isis, and the arch symbolizing the lunar cycle all belong to the moon goddess. She symbolizes the image-making and illumination of the feminine energy. Her blue robes are set off against a curtain illustrating the Tree of Life, showing that her power derives from her position on the central pillar of the tree.

She is open and changeable, wise and dark, not judgmental as she is able to identify with both poles of all feelings, shown by the crescent foundation and the black and white columns. She signifies the unpredictable and contrary ways by which the soul expresses its uniting intelligence.

ABOVE MANY OF THE IMAGES ASSOCIATED WITH THE HIGH PRIESTESS (FOR EXAMPLE THE ISIS CROWN) ARE ALSO SYMBOLS OF THE MOON.

GUIDED IMAGERY

'You wander through the forest, further and further away from the city. The flowing stream that accompanies you in the journey snakes around and you find yourself upon a plateau surrounded by the swirling waters. Boarding a moored boat you travel down the stream of consciousness, as you do so being invaded by visions of past and future. The awesome banks on either side are present truths, bounding your journey and defining your path. Although out of control in the dark waters, you bring new insight into the shadows you have always feared within yourself. The torch you carry sheds light on your own unconscious source of wisdom and power. In the heart of darkness you find your own light. You juggled life, but now your knowing arises from within yourself.'

THE MEANING

Hidden life truths that are revealed through intuition, divination, feminine wisdom and revelation. Taking emotional chances; foresight; fluctuation; forces of nature and psychic or artistic abilities. Inspired silence and secrecy; healing magic; walking the path of destiny. Emotional balance derived from foresight; overwhelming enthusiasm.

AFFIRMATION

'In searching my inner darkness I discover the foundation of my outer knowing. My integrity grows from intuition and perception.'

THE EMPRESS

DAUGHTER OF THE MIGHTY ONES

ARCANUM THREE
THE PLANET VENUS
KEY WORD: NATURE

THE EMPRESS.

The beautiful Empress holds a sceptre of physical dominion and sits upon her pillow throne that bears a shield decorated with the symbol of Venus. She sits within her protected domain of ripened corn, cypress trees and rushing water as the goddess of fertility and abundance, and her head, crowned with the 12 stars, shows her as mistress of the births of all souls. She bestows love and life, and also takes them away. She represents the wilderness of the instincts, which must be subdued and nurtured to promote fruitfulness.

THE SYMBOLIC EMPRESS

She is fecundity and the joyful love of all living things and the gateway into the world of form, but also contains sorrowful power over the dark mysteries of death. Her red throne denotes pure instinct and her robe is covered with pomegranates of universal integration. Her power emerges from the unconscious and she activates the deep emotional core of all beings. Her upturned lunar crescent and wheat sheaf show that maturity requires leaving the protection of the mother, and that sacrifice is required to dominate instinctual nature.

GUIDED IMAGERY

'As you walk through the field of ripe wheat, the golden grain stretches as far as you can see, bounded only by distant mountain ranges. Birds sing, bees buzz and you can smell myriad flowers and hear the growth all around you. Everything is joy and abundance. You approach a towering cypress tree that penetrates the edge of a deep, clear pool of water, its roots rending the dark, rich soil and emerging from the dark water. You feel the presence of a radiant mother-bride near, bestowing her blessings and love on you and fertilizing your actions performed in her honour. As you lie upon the fragrant soil, you feel as though you could stay forever in the protection of the womb of nature and her goddesses.'

THE MEANING

The path of harmony through emotional conflict. Fruitfulness and fertility and their relationship to attachment and physical value. Creating life leads to the death of your previous state, and openness to your natural acts can bring closer contacts, but also vulnerability. Try to integrate and harmonize with others.

AFFIRMATION

'I nurture my creative potential as a gateway for my highest personal fulfilment. I give love and support to others to express my feeling of inner peace, and accept their beauty and affection with wisdom.'

THE EMPEROR

THE EMPEROR.

SON OF THE MORNING

CHIEF AMONG THE MIGHTY
ARCANUM FOUR
THE SIGN ARIES
KEY WORD: LAW

The crowned Emperor sits on his cubic throne with ram's head carvings holding an ankh-surmounted sceptre and a globe. He is the lord of thought and action, parent, with the Empress, of the Fool. Pure will is his instrument, and intuition his battle plan.

33

THE SYMBOLIC EMPEROR

The Emperor is the power of Aries, the first emanation from the Empress and the self-assertiveness of the will and power over instincts. The cubic throne against the backdrop of mountains is his anchor in the physical world, the body and domain of the earth mother, over which the masculine will attempts to assert its power. The organization of his power is impressed upon the powerful feminine unconscious. He is a spiritual warrior and his truth ultimately triumphs over physical power alone.

ABOVE ARIES, THE SIGN OF THE RAM, IS ASSOCIATED WITH THE EMPEROR.

GUIDED IMAGERY

'Wandering in the harsh and barren wasteland, you come across a gigantic but deserted throne at the edge of a cool, clear lake. You climb into it, feel its authority and survey the view. Reflected in the gold around are symbols of power – a sceptre and orb, as well as weapons of battle. Suddenly you hear the sound of adoring subjects surrounding the throne and see readied armies preparing for battle awaiting your commands. They need your presence and direction, which you disperse with no hesitation. How do you feel being needed and respected for your power and wisdom?'

THE MEANING

Using will to conquer your unconsciousness. Recognizing the source of your strength of personality in mothering and nurturing. Confidence and creativity brought by taking chances. Following your own path and discovering the Way. Stability and power through taking on responsibility. Conviction with authority.

34

AFFIRMATION

'I have the willpower, discipline and ambition to take the first steps on the path to meet my highest goals.'

THE HIEROPHANT

MAGUS OF THE ETERNAL

ARCANUM FIVE

THE SIGN TAURUS

KEY WORD: RELIGION

Enthroned on a cube between two columns, the Hierophant wears a triple-tiered crown and holds a sceptre, surmounted by three crosses in his left hand. With his half-closed right hand he gives a benediction to two tonsured figures kneeling at his feet. Because he sits within a different temple from the High Priestess, he is the power of organized religion, whereas she symbolizes the esoteric. Before him are crossed keys and pentacles, indicating his domain over the physical world.

THE SYMBOLIC HIEROPHANT

The Hierophant has been called the Abbot, the High Priest and the Pope in his role as spiritual lawgiver. He is symbolic of the sign Taurus, the physical foundation of the spiritual quest, and is paired with, as he emanates from, the lunar High Priestess. He represents the integration of the concealed doctrine and its outer manifestation in his gesture and crossed keys, as he reveals daily the sacred aspects of life. Righteousness and rigidity are his inherent characteristics, yet he bestows grace to the bowing mendicants at his feet. The Hierophant is not religion, but its means of manifestation. The triple crown and crossed sceptre symbolize his ascent through the physical, emotional and mental worlds and his power of redemption.

ABOVE THE HIEROPHANT SYMBOLIZES THE RELIGIOUS NATURE WITHIN USE.

GUIDED IMAGERY

'Entering the dark and monumental halls of the ancient temple you feel overwhelmed and intimidated. A light glows from the far end of the colonnade as you behold a gigantic throne from which emanates a sense of spiritual power and piety. You mingle with a crowd of mendicants searching for blessing and grace, yet are singled out to receive the benediction of the crowned figure commanding the throne. What strikes you as remarkable is the contrasting shadow behind this figure, as though he draws his power from the darkness. He is a repository of wisdom and offers forgiveness, and unites pagan feelings with the clarity and light of Christ.'

THE MEANING

The ability to transform raw material into spiritual energies by acknowledging higher authority. Marriage or other higher alliances, mercy and benediction through servitude to higher powers. The value of ceremony and symbolism in mundane affairs. Art through practicality. Teaching and the ability to learn.

AFFIRMATION

'I am inspired and guided by my highest wisdom for the greatest good, finding it within myself and the world.'

THE LOVERS

THE LOVERS.

CHILDREN OF THE VOICE, ORACLE OF THE MIGHTY GODS

ARCANUM SIX
THE SIGN GEMINI
KEY WORD: EMOTIONAL LIFE

As a regent of the radiant sun, a winged figure from the clouds protects and nurtures a naked primordial couple in Eden, who are flanked by the Tree of Knowledge of Good and Evil and a fertile tree of life bearing 12 fruits. They are youthful and innocent, but have not yet consummated their union. The serpent beckons their attention as the world stretches out behind them to the highest mountains in the distance.

THE SYMBOLIC LOVERS

The Lovers are the communicative qualities of Gemini in their dual role as Eve and Adam or sister and brother, signifying the two forms of male-female relationship that integrate in every couple and within each individual of both sexes. The female-male duality emanates from the One above, and by implication the path of knowledge requires the reuniting of these apparent opposites. The feminine powers of the unconscious and of time nurture and yet conquer all relationships. Desire may put knowledge and fertility in their right relationship as the focus of cosmic forces above us.

ABOVE OUR EMOTIONAL LIFE, INCLUDING OUR FRIENDSHIPS AND RELATIONSHIPS, ARE CENTRAL THEMES OF THE LOVERS CARD.

GUIDED IMAGERY

'The garden stretches as far as you can see, lush and fertile in every way. Plants blossom and fruit before your eyes, and everything is lit with golden sunlight. In a radiant clearing are two trees, one with 12 different ripe fruits hanging from its branches, the other beautiful beyond description but containing a glittering green serpent. The allure of the trees is difficult to resist, and the promise of knowingness emanates from the serpent, making his presence quite seductive. An image of your ideal partner appears before you, encouraging your fantasies and hopes of perfect union. By letting go your resistance, your wishes will be answered.'

THE MEANING

Higher aspects of yourself can be the best mediators. Value the process more than the outcome. Choices between outer and inner worth. Control brings higher awareness. Attraction and vacillation may only be resolved by decision and commitment. Friendly or brotherly-sisterly communication, friendship between opposites united in knowledge; intellectual flexibility.

AFFIRMATION

'I love both my feminine and the masculine parts, and wish to share my integration with others by showing how accepting I can be.'

THE CHARIOT

CHILD OF THE POWERS OF THE WATERS, LORD OF THE TRIUMPH OF LIGHT

ARCANUM SEVEN
THE SIGN CANCER
KEY WORD: MAGIC

THE CHARIOT.

The handsome and upright man rides in his war chariot drawn by two sphinxes, one white and the other black. The double wand of his powerful will, which tames the instincts and emotions, is pointing upwards from within the chariot. The charioteer's helmet, together with the canopy above his head, are decorated with stars. He wears crescent moons on his shoulders and the zodiacal belt that lies loosely around his waist indicates his celestial and heavenly purpose. On the front of the chariot body is painted a winged solar disc and a representation of the linga and yoni (the male and females sexual organs), linking female and male energies. The walled city away from which he travels indicates the world of form that he leaves behind in his quest to dominate the divine realm within himself.

ABOVE THE CHARIOT IS LINKED TO THE ZODIAC SIGN OF CANCER. INTERPRETING THE CARD ASTROLOGICALLY HELPS US TO GAIN A DEEPER UNDERSTANDING OF ITS SYMBOLISM.

THE SYMBOLIC CHARIOT

The Chariot is the dominance of the awakened mind over the instincts and emotions symbolized by the sphinxes drawing him and the walled city that the charioteer has left behind. His Cancerian task is to break out of the captivity of feelings and to conquer in the outer world that which he has overcome in his inner world. The cubic shape of the chariot and its four canopy supports symbolize the body and its fourfold nature. The canopy decorated with stars and the two black and white sphinxes signify our contradictory animal and divine nature and refer to the celestial hierarchy of constellations that reflect earthly actions. The secret wisdom is attained by warring with and overcoming our lower nature and bringing the resultant unified being into the world of form.

GUIDED IMAGERY
'You are a warrior of light, wearing shining armour emblazoned with crescent moons and strange glyphs, climbing into your gleaming chariot. You leave the darkened city of your birth behind as you must respect and embrace the earthly realm where you were dominated by mother and senses. The sphinxes drawing your cubic chariot are powerfully pulling in opposite directions, awaiting your controlling will. As you take the reins, they unite with great force along the clear path until they ascend towards the twinkling stars above. The starry canopy of your vehicle disappears against the heavens, and you accept that their and your place is to merge with the constellations. Knowing the loving core within you, you ascend to the place of higher understanding.'

THE MEANING
Understanding that arises from emotional difficulty. The path of renouncing earthly power in favour of personal integration. Conquering one's instincts and directing oneself wisely. Obeying the higher level of being within ourselves. Irreversible power acknowledged from above.

AFFIRMATION
'I conquer my instincts and emotions with the intentions of my higher self and achieve physical goals.'

STRENGTH

STRENGTH.

DAUGHTER OF THE FLAMING SWORD, LEADER OF THE LION

ARCANUM EIGHT

THE SIGN LEO

KEY WORD: SELF-CONSCIOUSNESS

An innocent young woman, wearing a crown and belt of flowers, closes the jaws of a lion. Above her head is suspended a lemniscate, the infinity symbol of the holy spirit. She has yoked the savage beast with a chain of flowers, showing that she has subdued her animalistic passions and overcome the lower aspects of her nature in favour of her higher self.

THE SYMBOLIC STRENGTH

Strength is symbolized by the sign Leo in its virginal and moral self-consciousness and spirituality, albeit in a primarily unconscious form. The lemniscate echoes the Magician in its taming of the self. Strength emanates from a life of contemplation, of integrating with the chain of souls, shown by the flowers. Some relate her to the goddess Diana, with her arrows of organization and direction of creativity, conquering the destructive influence of desire and sexuality. The divine laws of love and strength are bound to prevail over the wild instincts.

GUIDED IMAGERY

'In the hot and rocky place you wander without water and sustenance. As the only way out is through a narrow canyon, you enter and see a ferocious lion blocking your way. To run or hide would be fruitless, so the only solution is to walk slowly and calmly towards the lion, trusting your good heart to tame the savage beast. Your confidence affects him as he moves to you, not in anger or violence, but as a friend. He brushes against your leg like a house cat and presents his head to be stroked. You realize that in your centredness you have made a potential enemy into an ally and source of spiritual strength.'

THE MEANING
The courage to face fears brings great personal power. Spirit is capable of overcoming unconscious blocks and repression. Conquering the self is the greatest battle. Action, success and honour, courage and consciousness of self.

AFFIRMATION
'My greatest fears and weakness provide the energy that enables me to express my higher self and reach my dreams.'

41

THE HERMIT

PROPHET OF THE ETERNAL,
MAGUS OF THE VOICE OF POWER

THE HERMIT.

ARCANUM NINE
THE SIGN VIRGO
KEY WORD: SEARCHING WISDOM

On the apex of a mountain chain, a cloaked and bearded old man carrying a long staff and a lamp, illuminated by a star, searches for the truth. Although he is alone in his meditation on the natural world, the Hermit brings enlightenment and openness to the barren reaches of the Earth and initiates the journey across the valley of life.

THE SYMBOLIC HERMIT

The Hermit expresses the Virgo qualities of purity and discrimination, as his simplicity is transformed into understanding through maturity. His lonely search is symbolized in some decks by the partial obscuring of the lantern, which implies obedience to the hidden doctrine, but it may also mean recognition and wisdom from stellar influences. The mysteries are protected from the uninitiated by the isolation and loneliness of its practitioners.

GUIDED IMAGERY

'Trekking across the harsh mountain range you reach a small but high plateau that presents a magnificent view over the surrounding countryside. Suspended on top between a barren tree and a fruitful tree is a rainbow of silk, flapping in the wind, through which the rising sun shines, illuminating you in spectral colours. In this quiet and isolated place your mood instantly changes from hopelessness to positive expectation, and you feel as though you have found the inner strength in your meditative isolation to continue on to your highest goals.'

THE MEANING

Meditation and the inward path allow everything to be seen more clearly. Hidden meanings may be discovered through perseverance and open-ness. Service and renunciation bring wisdom. Naivety and prudishness. Circumspection, caution and distance from feelings. Purity and discrimination.

LEFT TIME SPENT IN MEDITATION BRINGS CLARITY TO ANY SITUATION. LIKE THE HERMIT, WE NEED TO LOOK INWARD FROM TIME TO TIME.

AFFIRMATION

'I look within for the guidance of my higher self to elevate my moods and direct me to the light.'

WHEEL OF FORTUNE

LORD OF THE FORCES OF LIFE

ARCANUM 10
THE PLANET JUPITER
KEY WORD: LIFE

A sphinx armed with a sword is astride the Wheel of Fortune, rotating perpetually like the eternal cycle of life in the universe. Magical symbols identify the eight spokes of the wheel, and the letters spelling ROTA, a transliteration of TARO, and the Hebrew name of God – '*Yod he vau he*' – are inscribed around the rim of the wheel. The Egyptian god Typhon rises up the left side and the snake of time falls down the right side of the figure. In the corners sit the four beasts of Ezekiel, or the Apocalypse, the bull, the lion, the eagle and the man, all opening the books of the law.

THE SYMBOLIC WHEEL OF FORTUNE

The planet Jupiter transcends time as it rules higher mind and the spiritual life. The half-lion, half-human sphinx symbolizes equilibrium derived from integrating the lower animal nature with the higher mind. The Indian wheel of samsara is the cycle of birth, death and rebirth upon which all souls are crucified, bound by the mechanics of the zodiac, symbolized by the four sacred beasts, which are also the four signs of the fixed cross – Taurus, Leo, Scorpio and

Aquarius. The creatures of time, Typhon and the snake, show that time runs the wheel. The only liberation lies within the centre, in the domain of the self.

GUIDED IMAGERY

'Rotating solemnly through the starry expanses of space, the eternal wheel carries the life principle round and round. Wild beasts, creatures of beauty and power, and humans crawl perpetually around the wheel and attempt to fight against gravity and climb along one of the eight spokes into the centre, which glows with the white light of salvation. The need to hold on tightly to avoid falling off counteracts the desire to move quickly towards the goal. The need to touch and crawl over the threatening or repulsive animals makes you feel ill and under constant threat. Suddenly you let go your grasp which, instead of spinning you into the void, guides you toward the magical temple at the centre of life. By releasing, you find peace.'

44

THE MEANING

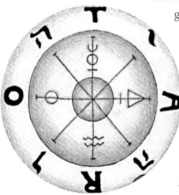

ABOVE THE EIGHT SPOKES OF THE WHEEL EACH
HAVE A MAGIC SYMBOL AND ON THE OUTER
CIRCLE, LETTERS SPELL OUT 'ROTA', A
TRANSLITERATION OF 'TARO'.

Understanding the process of time brings a greater integration with the forces of destiny. Taking chances leads to success, but also to occasional failure, in keeping with the dynamics of the wheel. The laws of karma bring wisdom and peace. Good fortune, success, luck, unpredictable influences.

AFFIRMATION

'As I experience the fluctuations of my physical, emotional and mental life and accept the process completely, I am able to manifest my full spiritual potential.'

JUSTICE

DAUGHTER OF THE LORDS OF TRUTH, RULER OF THE BALANCE

ARCANUM 11

THE SIGN LIBRA

KEY WORD: TRUTH

Crowned Justice sits between her pillars holding scales for weighing guilt or innocence and a sword to administer her verdict. The image is similar to the Egyptian god Osiris who weighs souls before their trip to the underworld. The principle of balance and adjustment implies the recognition of a higher moral and spiritual order that must be considered against the mundane life where such considerations are of little importance.

THE SYMBOLIC JUSTICE

The Libran goddess Justice shows that the feminine principle is a source of balance and integration. As the goddess Astraea, she personifies virtue and the recognition of partnership and relationship. The suspended pans carry the opposing aspects of the self while the scales themselves mediate between them, signifying the third principle or viewpoint that arbitrates between them. An awareness of one's own inner imbalances must precede integration with others or outer reality. Partners are either defined or limited by the laws of their relationship, and the future of their lives bears witness to their ability to make just choices.

GUIDED IMAGERY

'Entering the massive and impressive halls of black and white marble it is clear that you will be judged by superior powers that care not for your emotional stances or excuses. A cold sweat arises at the realization that this place is a house of justice but also of retribution and death. Above the scarlet dais is suspended a gigantic golden scales, delicately poised in space, awaiting the breath of a feather to disturb its equilibrium. You are afraid to breathe for fear that you will be responsible for the terrible onslaught of divine right. Realizing that you do not have a fear of the truth brings a clearing of the air and an alignment with these superior intelligences.'

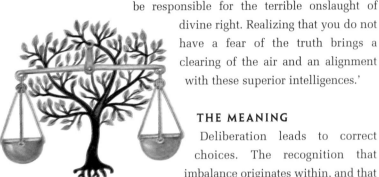

ABOVE BALANCED SCALES ARE A SYMBOL OF JUSTICE AND JUDGEMENT. THE JUSTICE CARD IN A READING MAY IMPLY THAT THERE IS IMBALANCE IN OUR LIFE.

THE MEANING

Deliberation leads to correct choices. The recognition that imbalance originates within, and that the restoration of balance also begins within. Harmony, equality, justice, getting just deserts, legal affairs.

AFFIRMATION

'I am balanced and able to understand the outer manifestations of my inner issues, and subsequently I am able to take the correct action with honour.'

THE HANGED MAN

SPIRIT OF THE MIGHTY WATERS

ARCANUM 12
THE PLANET NEPTUNE AND THE ELEMENT WATER
KEY WORD: SACRIFICE

A smiling golden-haired young man with a halo hangs from living branches shaped like a *tau* cross. His legs form a cross and his arms

extend behind his back, making an upside down triangle – his whole body makes the alchemical sulphur symbol signifying the eternal fire. His countenance suggests suspended animation rather than martyrdom.

THE SYMBOLIC HANGED MAN

Water symbolizes the emotional life and the Hanged Man is pure unconsciousness. He appears to be sacrificed by those on earth, but is, in reality, showing his allegiance to the powers above. Neptune is the visionary psychic domain, which is more vivid than reality – spiritual humanity is trapped by reality, crucified on the cross of matter. The Hebrew letter *tau* is the saturnine quality of time and signifies the entrapment of the world. The pure soul understands and loves its boundaries like an adoring mother loves her child.

GUIDED IMAGERY

'Feeling trapped by the limitations of your own conscious image of the universe, you wish to move beyond these restrictions. The meditative position you adopt is a headstand without supporting arms, and once you achieve this position you begin to feel the transformation taking place. What were before glittering stars in the unlimited heavens above, now seem dense and lifeless, while the gravitational bond of the solid and impermeable earth below becomes alive with vibrant energy and illumination. You can feel your head radiating an other-worldly light in your ultimate enchantment.'

ABOVE WATER, WHICH SYMBOLIZES EMOTIONAL LIFE, IS THE ELEMENT ATTRIBUTED TO THE HANGED MAN.

THE MEANING

The secrets of divination and prophecy lie within the self and can be revealed through communication with the feminine and unconscious aspects of the self. Wisdom comes through sacrifice, trials, being circumspect.

AFFIRMATION

'I relinquish my attachments and fears in the faith that this sacrifice of invalid patterns will open me to a new life.'

DEATH

CHILD OF THE GREAT TRANSFORMATION, LORD OF THE GATES OF DEATH

ARCANUM 13
THE SIGN SCORPIO
KEY WORD: DEATH

A skeleton in armour is mounted on a white horse. He carries his black banner emblazoned with an inverted red rose through a field containing a fallen king, a sleeping maiden, a kneeling lad and a praying prelate awaiting his doom. The tranquil river of life flows nearby and through the twin towers on the horizon, the sun's last rays blaze.

THE SYMBOLIC DEATH

Death overshadows all aspects of life and is omnipresent in its process of testing, separation and renewal. Death's mount shows the animal and instinctive reality of dying, while his banner signifies the eternal qualities of life that emerge from apparent destruction.

Despite the finality of transformation, the river of life flows on and the sun of immortality shines through the gateway symbolizing the dualism of this ultimate challenge.

GUIDED IMAGERY

'Standing in a state of cold and still detachment, your body seems to fall away. Its heaviness, caused by worldly burdens and emotional attachments, begins to lessen as its feelings leave. The long journey begins, initially with sadness and regret, but gradually the glimmering soul detaches from the body and rises, seeking the white light above and beyond. Upon this star your soul's journey is now focused, the inner light overshadowing the outer pain of living. The release is a godsend, a rest from holding on to decaying patterns, the start of a new adventure. You can see the small physical world left behind, while the greater world of spirit beckons. There nothing but darkness, here eternal sun. You have been crucified within your body, but now you are free.'

49

THE MEANING

Death represents change of some kind – a period of transition, loss and renewal. Breakdown leading to transformation. Letting go – the releasing of possessions, ideas or relationships or, alternatively, releasing old ways of seeing oneself or other people.

BELOW RISING AND SETTING EACH DAY, THE SUN IS A SYMBOL OF IMMORTALITY. IT APPEARS ON THE HORIZON IN THE DEATH CARD, REPRESENTING THE DUALISM OF THIS CARD.

AFFIRMATION

'I leave my needs and relationships behind and seek the higher light that is within myself. The more I let go, the freer and more luminous I will become.'

TEMPERANCE

TEMPERANCE.

DAUGHTER OF THE RECONCILERS, BRINGER FORTH OF LIFE

ARCANUM 14

THE SIGN SAGITTARIUS

KEY WORD: INTEGRATION

A heavenly, winged angel with a solar disc headband pours the mercurial life substance from a golden to a silver chalice. Upon her flowing robes is a triangle within a square. One foot rests upon the earth and the other in the life-giving water, at the intersection of which many plants and flowers grow. Stretching away from this fertile source curves a road leading to a crown-shaped light blazing beyond the hills.

THE SYMBOLIC TEMPERANCE

Temperance is the quality that characterizes the integration of the lower fertile animal instincts and the higher need for transcendental consciousness. Sagittarius is the moral aspiration and craving to understand that leads the soul beyond sensual satisfaction to the higher psychic and spiritual life. The transformative Aquarian fluid shows the necessary flow of masculine conscious and feminine unconscious qualities that together create the integrated Self. The vessels are wombs of the potential creativity of our outer and inner being that require interaction and the exchange of energies. The Greek goddess Persephone similarly bridged life and death by nourishing the souls below preceding their rebirth. The goal of the process of integration is beyond the horizon, in the domain of the higher being.

ABOVE SAGITTARIUS, WHICH
IS IDENTIFIED WITH TEMPERANCE, LEADS THE SOUL
TO A HIGHER PSYCHIC AND SPIRITUAL LIFE.

GUIDED IMAGERY

'Arising from the Death of my clarity, from within the golden vessel you spiral slowly towards its mouth, and arch out into the clear, fresh air, only to be caught by another silvery grail. Your fluidity arises from the crystal lake and emerges onto the fertile and damp ground. You are surrounded by lush and beautiful plants, reeds and flowery stalks that grow upwards towards the blue sky above. You feel drawn to follow the meandering stream to its source beyond the mountains, in the exalted realm where sky and earth intermingle. Your unity lies above and beyond you, yet its feeling always exists within when you achieve and recognize your natural balance.'

THE MEANING

Finding a balance between outer and inner moderation defines new limits. Life moves perpetually through phases of light and dark, active and passive. Identification with the flow. Patience, self-control and accommodation are required for integration. Circumspection despite physical demands. Psyche and body find a path of integration.

AFFIRMATION

'I integrate and blend the diverse polarities of my life to create balance, unity and harmony in creating who I am and manifesting what I do.'

THE DEVIL

LORD OF THE GATES OF MATTER, CHILD OF THE FORCES OF TIME

ARCANUM 15

THE SIGN CAPRICORN

KEY WORD: MATERIALISM

The horned goat with wings of a bat stands on a altar, an inverted pentangle on his forehead. One hand is raised in devilish benediction and the other points a phallic torch toward the ground. Upon his navel sits a hermetic caduceus symbol instead of sexual organs. Chained to his cubic altar of grey stone by their necks are two small figures, a male and female. They have horns and tails, reminding us of the bestial and unconscious natures of Adam and Eve after their Fall from Grace in the Garden of Eden.

THE SYMBOLIC DEVIL

Capricorn is the corruption of mechanistic materialism and the enchainment of temptation. The god Pan requires indulgence and wild abandonment to the lowest instincts, and the chains show the bondage resulting from the worship of such inferior energies. Weak and corruptible humanity, signified by the two figures, is trapped and dominated by this masked Devil who gives false benediction and demeans the flame of spiritual understanding. He is the tempting Guardian of the Threshold, past whom the initiate must pass on the route to enlightenment.

GUIDED IMAGERY

'The dreary and dank cave smells of rotten animal carcasses and the sulphurous caverns below. Seeing a dim light flashing ahead, you enter into a subterranean chamber only to find you have been imprisoned by a great black beast, emblazoned with a flaming pentangle on his forehead. He offers the temptations of the flesh and worldly possessions in exchange for your immortal soul. You are punished almost to the point of accepting his offer, but suddenly a ray of light from a tiny opening in the chamber helps you realize that the material world is an illusion of which you are a part but that need not imprison you.'

THE MEANING

Overcoming the attractions of the physical world of the senses. The principle of self-centredness. Relationships to money and power. Excessive materialism prevents psychological growth. The difficulties caused by the demands and needs of the lower desires of the self.

AFFIRMATION

53

'I will transcend the chaos of my darkest fears and transform my weaknesses and vulnerabilities into a clear channel of light penetrating through the gloom.'

RIGHT GREED AND THE TEMPTATIONS OF THE MATERIAL WORLD MUST BE OVERCOME IF WE ARE TO ACHIEVE SELF-DEVELOPMENT.

THE TOWER

LORD OF THE HOSTS OF THE MIGHTY

ARCANUM 16

THE PLANET MARS

KEY WORD: THE FALL

Two figures, a male and female, are falling from a desolate stone tower. This tower, which is also called the House of God, is being struck by a bolt of lightning. The three windows are grouped with one higher than the other two, showing that the physical and emotional worlds are reconciled in the higher spiritual domain. The crown of the tower, which signifies spirituality as seen in the aura, and various bits of debris shower down from the violent event.

THE SYMBOLIC TOWER

The Martian energy of the tower is shattered by forced change, made manifest by the Scorpionic thunderbolt, which is both fate and forceful spirituality. The tower may represent the physical world or intellectual structures that we have erected, as well as the body and its state of health. Originally it was symbolic of the Fall of Adam and Eve or the destruction of the Tower of Babel. In either case the female and male figures are thrust apart, possibly through the sexual tensions of the phallic monument. Past patterns are shattered and the creative effort to modify them often requires the sacrifice of what formerly seemed secure. The 22 flaming *yods* (the Hebrew letter meaning work) show that from destruction come the forces of creativity and rebirth. The spirit of chaos rules the apparent order of the physical world.

GUIDED IMAGERY

'Amidst the steep and treacherous hills you approach the dark tower, immense in its solidity and strength. A wild and windy storm rages through the valleys, but orange fires burn within, illuminating its barred windows like portals into a furnace making gold from base metals. Suddenly a vivid shaft of zig-zagging lightning shatters the gloom and blasts the top of the tower from its base, spewing 22 flaming embers and tossing two brilliantly dressed figures into the

night sky. It is difficult to know whether they are escaping bondage or losing their security, such is the shock of the storm. You see them magically land, as though cushioned by their capes and velvet clothes. The storm abates and sunrise brings peace to the smoking ruin. You contemplate what you have seen.'

ABOVE THE TOWER CARD MAY SIGNIFY OPPRESSION, CONFLICT AND CHAOS IN CLOSE PERSONAL RELATIONSHIPS.

THE MEANING

Total change signalled by the end of previous patterns, leading to new beginnings. Unexpected disruptions are caused when attempting to protect oneself leading to feelings of vulnerability. An inability to look at inner unrest and suppressed anger. Past relationships are abandoned and changes of opinion prevent reconciliation. Downfall, losing everything, violence, sexual domination, insecurity.

AFFIRMATION

'Sudden realizations about inadequate past ideas and patterns free me instantly from self-created limitations and physically binding circumstances.'

THE STAR

DAUGHTER OF THE FIRMAMENT, DWELLER BETWEEN THE WATERS

ARCANUM 17

THE SIGN AQUARIUS

KEY WORD: ASTRAL RELIGION

A radiant star of eight rays is surrounded by seven lesser stars. A young and beautiful naked woman kneels on the land but her foot is in the water. She pours the waters of life onto the land and in the sea, providing life-giving sustenance to both. In a tree behind her sits a bird.

56

THE SYMBOLIC STAR

The Aquarian symbolism of the star is idealistic, utopian and perfect in form, like the unveiled truth she represents. The maiden guides the goals of humanity and shines with ethereal light. Progressive spiritual evolution and the necessity for grounding integrate, symbolized by the two vessels and her stance astride water and land. The central star is Sirius, worshipped by the Egyptians as the sun of our sun, and the seven stars of the Great Bear are the governing esoteric spirits of our universe, just as the star symbolizes the soul. Astrological influences nurture human expectations. New conceptions and opportunities arise through the feminine desire for synthesis.

GUIDED IMAGERY

'Wandering through the barren valley at sunset, you pray for some sign of life. Turning past a small hill with a tree surmounting it, you hear a bird calling and see a cool, clear pond surrounded by fertility everywhere, in the water, at its edge and in the proliferation of wildlife around it. The intersection between the water and land has a magical radiance, and the surface of the water glistens like gold and silver. The atmosphere is tranquil and quiet, and you feel nurtured, supported and full of eternal hope for the future without knowing why. As the sky darkens you notice the gigantic star overhead, surrounded by seven others, dancing across the heavens. Suddenly you know that you are protected by forces beyond yourself.'

THE MEANING

Barren areas of your life may be fertilized by seeing the power above. Prayer brings release and accesses the depths of your psyche. Faith and hope guide the present. A symbol of the collective unconscious. Questing for realization. The magical power of astrology representing higher powers. Hope and expectation.

AFFIRMATION

'I am a living, breathing star radiating pure energies and giving sustenance to myself and others through the inspiration of my light.'

57

THE MOON

RULER OF FLUX AND REFLUX

ARCANUM 18
THE SIGN PISCES
KEY WORD: ASTROLOGICAL NATURE

A dog and a wolf bay at the crescent moon. In the distance, on either side of the meandering path, lie two dark towers. The face of the waxing moon gleams as it cries fertilizing dewdrops onto the ground below. A large red lobster emerges from the lapping waters of the unconscious onto dry land.

THE MOON.

THE SYMBOLIC MOON

Pisces symbolizes the psychic and sacrificial qualities of the moon goddess. It was believed that her tears fertilized the land, and the duality of her nature is shown by the two towers and baying animals, representing the unconscious voices we all hear through emotional veils. The towers are rigid symbols of masculine, phallic consciousness, through which the unconscious penetrates as through a transparent veil. The moon counsels balanced feelings as an equilibrating path between the dualistic upper and lower worlds. The pond is the past, stagnant below us, and out of which our higher self emerges as the lobster.

GUIDED IMAGERY

'The boat crossed the dark lake and grounded ashore – it had been mystically guided here. Walking up the shore, the beginning of a path below is reflected in a glowing cleft in the cloudy sky overhead. As you walk up the gradual incline the clouds part and through the heavy air the brilliant crescent moon shines its fertilizing rays down onto your expectant face. The path ahead meanders between two sinister and dark towers, standing sentinel over the only way ahead. As you move carefully, you are shocked to hear the baying of a wild dog and a wolf echoing through the mist. Your need to continue overcomes your fears at what could lie ahead. As you keep unwaveringly along the path and simply acknowledge but resist the dangers lurking you see, over a rise, the road ahead, stretching clearly towards the distant horizon.'

THE MEANING

Deceptions arouse strong emotions and must be clarified. Past influences stand in the way of progress and development. Meditation and inner light compensate for outer illusions and unrealistic expectations from the world. Obscurity and trickery. Warnings from others and from intuitions. A multitude of influences can lead to confusion and incorrect priorities.

AFFIRMATION

'I value both my positive and negative feelings as expressions of the world around me, and I accept their enrichment and fertilization.'

THE SUN

LORD OF THE FIRE OF THE WORLD

ARCANUM 19
THE SUN
KEY WORD: VISIBLE EXPERIENCE

The brilliant noonday sun casts its golden rays down into an enclosed garden, surrounded by tall sunflowers. A young naked child, carrying a huge scarlet banner, is mounted on a beautiful white horse. The light of the world, carried by children, reflects the creative child that is within us all. Consciousness and spirit penetrate all enclosures, bringing both awareness and knowledge.

THE SYMBOLIC SUN

The sun is the source of spiritual energy, creativity and life, expressing itself as a beneficent and protective god above us. The image has also been seen as Sirius, the dog star of the Egyptians shown in the Star, bestowing fertility through the goddess Isis.

ABOVE THE POWER OF THE SUN IS DEPICTED AS A SOLAR DISC IN THE CROWN OF THE EGYPTIAN GODDESS ISIS.

The more powerful the draw or demands of the physical world, the more important is penetration of high spiritual wisdom. The integration of above and below happens within the yearly cycle of the twelve signs of the zodiac, bringing the alternation of life and death on earth.

GUIDED IMAGERY

'Within the masonry enclosure the cold morning air brings a sense of barrenness. But when the sun rises above the wall's blockage, a supernatural warmth arises gradually and warms and nurtures your body and brings excitement and inspiration to your mind. A feeling of belonging to this powerful and yet totally controlled being above echoes the entrapment of your body and the acceptance of your destiny, written in the skies but enacted through the alliance with your free will to act.

A mystical child, taming a wild horse that bursts into the courtyard, makes you think of your ability to control the unconscious impulses you have by the recognition of your conscious control over the world. What you think is what you are.'

ABOVE IF THE SUN CARD APPEARS IN OUR READING, IT MAY SIGNIFY THE SUCCESSFUL OUTCOME OF CREATIVE PROJECTS.

THE MEANING

The awakening of the child within the individual brings new life, joy and inspiration. Higher influences bring freedom from the rigid structures and the demands of the physical world. The merging of two people requires a binding and integration of their higher ideals. Experiencing life in the sun activates inner truth and increases your self worth. Happiness, contentment and success are in abundance.

AFFIRMATION

'I fully understand my physical limitations but look to heaven to help me find the inspiration to trust and live with my inner child. Personal growth will come through relinquishing my rigid personal boundaries.'

JUDGEMENT

SPIRIT OF PRIMAL FIRE

ARCANUM 20
THE PLANET PLUTO AND
THE ELEMENT FIRE
KEY WORDS: REGENERATION AND
RESURRECTION

An angel appears from the clouds blowing a bannered trumpet bearing a cross. Below it the dead are rising from their watery graves. In the foreground stand a triumvirate of man, child and woman with outstretched hands, as though welcoming the resurrection. The Biblical Last Judgement portrays the resurrection of the souls of those blessed in the eyes of God, a concept depicted here.

THE SYMBOLIC JUDGEMENT

The function of the element fire is to provide heat and energy when controlled, and total destruction when rampant. The force of life here needs the degeneration and breakdown into component parts before resurrection can take place. Only the death of obsolete life structures and beliefs allows the rebirth into higher, more transcendent states of consciousness. The coffins are the body, in which we are imprisoned until liberated at death, and they float upon the surface of the unconscious awaiting the awakening. Integration between female

ABOVE FIRE IS THE ELEMENT OF THE JUDGEMENT CARD, FIRE CAN BOTH CREATE AND DESTROY.

and male brings the inner child to birth and allows unification. The angel above is Gabriel giving a celestial justification to the reality of resurrection.

GUIDED IMAGERY

'Among the snow-capped mountain fastnesses and the enclosed valley, ringed with drifting eagles, you come upon a plain somewhere between earth and heaven. It is the graveyard of mortal souls, but contains the great potential of rebirth. The grey sky and barren ground begin a profound transformation before your eyes. The earth breaks up of its own accord, and long-closed coffin lids push the surface of the ground away, as the sky turns brilliant blue and the plants and flowers push through the ground and reach toward the sky. The time of resurrection is at hand, and the souls of the dead stretch and pay homage to the heavenly host above, who symbolize their rebirth. The joy of creation and transcendence reigns over the valley.'

THE MEANING

Forgiveness and repentance bring about resurrection into a new life. Making central choices reinforces the correctness of your spiritual direction. Completion and resolution can only create redemption. Changes of position and beliefs. Rebirth. Being judged reflects your judgements of others. Success comes through decisiveness.

AFFIRMATION

'I release my feelings of bodily bondage and sense the awakening of my soul as my integration process brings a perpetual flowering in its wake.'

THE WORLD

GREAT ONE OF THE NIGHT OF TIME

ARCANUM 21
THE PLANET SATURN
KEY WORD: TIME

The four creatures of the Apocalypse and Ezekiel's vision are grouped around the oval garland of flowers bound above and below with crossed red ribbons. Within a maiden dances, enwrapped with violet silk and carrying a wand in each hand. She is the scarlet woman dancing the dance of time and eternity, spiralling and twirling through life as a blithe spirit.

THE SYMBOLIC WORLD

The spiralling bonds of Saturn define and limit physical space and time, the oval vessel within which the dance of life takes place. Fertility and sexuality exist to propagate the universe and create the manifest world, providing the players in the divine plan. The opposing crosses are the duality and conflict engendered by the existence of life, yet the battle takes place within. The spiritual process of discovery begins with the Fool and ends here in the heavens, where its markers are astrological as well as astronomical, religious and secular. The world is the father of form and also takes away what he bestows upon all forms of intelligence. That is his function and the ultimate mystery.

GUIDED IMAGERY

'Drifting through the dark and cold vastness of space, piloting against unmeasurable and unimaginable clusters of galaxies and backgrounds of the void, you enter a sacred domain. A spiral of stars swirls in an oval form around and around, its boundaries clearly alive with the animals, objects and beings of the zodiac belt. Their presence can be felt, as though instead of stars they are the bodies of these mythic creatures from whom our lives are created. At the centre of their swirling movement, instead of the outer coldness is a warmth, a golden glow arising from a dancing goddess, spinning and leaping in supremely beautiful arcs, wearing only a glimmer of a violet silken cloth draped around her as the wings of an angel. As you come closer, the goddess glides near and whispers in your ear the key to enlightenment.'

THE MEANING

Our sense of well-being originates from the ability to understand the whole; the need for integration of personal and collective; encouraging self-trust and dominance; the primary principle of individuation; expressions of identification in the world; creating or building a new vision of yourself.

AFFIRMATION

'I am a co-creator of the world, and know that I will be nurtured and supported by it as I acknowledge my identity with all its actions.'

THE MINOR ARCANA

CHAPTER FIVE

U ntil the creation of the Rider-Waite pack in this century, the court cards and Minor Arcana cards of the tarot were similar to playing cards. The court cards had similar images of kings, queens, knights and pages holding the symbols of the four suits. The Minor Arcana cards, with their numbers of pentacles, swords, cups or wands, were similar to the pips on playing cards. There was no divinatory information at all in either the court cards or Minor Arcana.

THE THREE CLASSES OF TAROT CARDS

There is a hierarchy of strength and value in the three classes of tarot cards. The 22 Major Arcana cards, being archetypes, are the strongest. The 16 court card, which are character types representing the archetypal energies, are the next strongest. Finally, the cards numbered from ace to 10 in each of the four suits are a sequence of events through which the archetypes come into being in day-to-day situations. The tarot, therefore, embodies three levels of operation:

Major Arcana = archetypal influences = depth psychology work
Court Cards = character or personality types
    = sub-personality work
Numbered Cards = experiences and events = divinatory work

THE FOUR SUITS

The Minor Arcana is divided into four suits – wands, swords, cups and pentacles. The suits are symbolic of the ways that we function in life – the ways in which we sense and perceive the world, receive information and form inner intuitions, attempt to under-stand and adjust to the world and evaluate whether a given situation is pleasurable or not. These psychological functions are similar to, and derived

ABOVE FOUR SUITS (WANDS, SWORDS, CUPS, PENTACLES) MAKE UP THE TAROT DECK. EACH SUIT

HAS SPECIFIC QUALITIES AND IS ASSOCIATED WITH ONE OF THE FOUR ELEMENTS.

THE SUITS, ELEMENTS AND PSYCHOLOGICAL TYPES

The correspondences between suits, elements and psychological types have been made by many commentators, although there are differences of opinion about them. The most satisfying correlation is:

Wands	=	Fire Element	=	Intuition Type
Cups	=	Water Element	=	Feeling Type
Swords	=	Air Element	=	Thinking Type
Pentacles	=	Earth Element	=	Sensation Type

from, the four elements from which the Platonic philosophers, alchemists and astrologers believed the universe was made.

WANDS

The suit of wands corresponds to the element Fire, the first essential form of energy in the universe, emanating from the sun as rays of pure light that create life, yet are also capable of taking life. It was believed in ancient times that the universe began as 'cosmic fire' and that the essential, underlying life force or substance within all objects is fire. In daily life, the wands are life energy, individuality, insight, power of attainment and struggles, issues of success and failure, politics and commerce.

CUPS

The suit of cups corresponds to the element Water. The unusual way in which water flows into the form that contains it, and yet tends to break through all containers, is characteristic of its action. Water is

often seen as clear and transparent, but may also be dark, deep, mysterious and extremely dangerous when aroused. Duality and the quality of the shadow are inherent in the cup suit. It is water that symbolizes the unconscious, the source of all life, the most liquid, changeable, formless and yet powerful

ABOVE WATER, LIKE THE SUIT OF CUPS, IS FORMLESS, CONSTANTLY CHANGING. BOTH REPRESENT FLOWING EMOTIONS.

force in our world. The cups are also emotions and feelings, which are rhythmic, changeable, and take their form by whatever forces mould them. The element Water is symbolized by the cup that contains it. Its contents are understanding and consciousness. Thus the cup may be as evocative empty as full, and symbolic of our ability to contain as well as manage our feelings. In daily life, the cups mirror your emotional reality in matters of relationships, feelings, love, sex, romance, family, marriage and children.

SWORDS

The suit of swords corresponds to the element Air as the function of air is to cut through information in the act of discrimination. The element of Air symbolizes the principle of communication, of

the relationship of things to each other and to the higher and lower worlds. It is Air that brings together, but also that differentiates, criticizes, detaches from and alienates – in this sense it is unpredictable and unstable. In Eastern thought the mind must be stilled before the contemplative process of development can even begin. Images of mind often correlate its control with its capabilities. The mind makes us humane and sympathetic to others, but is also cold and detaches us from human concerns. In

ABOVE AIR IS THE EXPRESSION OF PURE MIND THAT MANIFESTS AS PERCEPTION, SELF-EXPRESSION, IDEOLOGY, COMPATIBILITY AND LOGIC.

daily life, the swords indicate the level of consciousness, and are ideas and their fulfilment, versatility, idealistic relationships, movement and changes of stance and mind.

PENTACLES

The suit of pentacles is associated with the element Earth. The pentacles were also called discs or coins, showing their connection with money and value. The pentacle was also the foremost protective talismanic figure in medieval times, thought to ward off evil spirits. It is earth from which all beings in the physical world arise, and is also the body through which our soul experiences the world. In the Christian mystery, the cross symbolizes both the world

ABOVE EARTH REPRESENTS ALL THAT IS SOLID AND TANGIBLE. IT DEFINES OUR RELATIONSHIP WITH THE PHYSICAL WORLD.

and the body into which we are incarnated. While the intuitional and thinking functions initiate activity, they must be grounded in reality through the Earth element. Earth stabilizes, sustains and defines, and represents our relationship with the tangible world and its boundaries. The ability to accept and work with the physical level is a prerequisite for the journey of enlightenment on the higher spiritual levels. In ancient societies, the body was often demeaned as evil or sinful, but its purification is essential to the entire process of integration. In daily life, the pentacles show what is happening in external reality – the physical body, money and our ability to use it, property and possessions, our practical and material side that is conservative and industrious. Pentacles are often resistant to change, are loyal and reliable, but can also be pig-headed, stubborn and unfeeling.

THE COURT CARDS

The court cards are associated with the elements and with the astrological signs in their function as personifications to be used in tarot, and as the symbols of the varying degrees of mastery of levels of consciousness.

The wands show intuitive and spiritual consciousness; the swords mental awareness; the cups emotional consciousness; and the pentacles, physical consciousness and external reality. In a psychological sense, the court cards may be understood as subpersonalities that indicate that a particular level of awareness has been obtained or is being required of us.

Crowley considered the court cards to be families of the four elements and their permutations. His correlation is interesting because it shows how the elements function within us, with each element containing aspects of the other three. (Crowley used the sequence knight, queen, prince and princess instead of the more traditional king, queen, knight and page.) The knight correlates with fire, the queen with water, the prince with air and the princess with earth. His sequence is therefore as follows:

THE COURT CARDS AND THE ELEMENTS

Knight of Wands	=	Fire of Fire	Intuitive intuition
Queen of Wands	=	Water of Fire	Emotional intuition
Prince of Wands	=	Air of Fire	Mental intuition
Princess of Wands	=	Earth of Fire	Physical intuition
Knight of Cups	=	Fire of Water	Intuitive feeling
Queen of Cups	=	Water of Water	Emotional feeling
Prince of Cups	=	Air of Water	Mental feeling
Princess of Cups	=	Earth of Water	Physical feeling
Knight of Swords	=	Fire of Air	Intuitive thinking
Queen of Swords	=	Water of Air	Emotional thinking
Prince of Swords	=	Air of Air	Intellectual thinking
Princess of Swords	=	Earth of Air	Physical thinking
Knight of Pentacles	=	Fire of Earth	Intuitive sensation
Queen of Pentacles	=	Water of Earth	Emotional sensation
Prince of Pentacles	=	Air of Earth	Mental sensation
Princess of Pentacles	=	Earth of Earth	Physical sensation

Within each psychological function are modes that correspond to the other functions. Thus the thoughts expressed by the Swords may arise from feelings in the case of the Queen of Swords, from intuitions in the case of the Knight or King of Swords, from the mind itself in the case of the Prince of Swords, and from the physical world or the body in the case of the Princess of Swords.

The four Kings, Queens and Knights are 'modes' of activity, transmitted through individuals around us and our own subpersonalities. When these cards are drawn in a reading, they signify the coming or presence of an individual who carries the

QUEEN of PENTACLES

ABOVE ASTROLOGICALLY, THE
QUEEN OF PENTACLES
CORRESPONDS TO THE CARDINAL
EARTH SIGN OF CAPRICORN.

archetype from whom we must see and accept its principles, or onto whom we project these qualities, and its presence requires that we exercise the level of mastery indicated.

Astrologically the four Kings, Queens and Knights correspond to the 12 sun signs of the zodiac. Astrology recognizes three modes of action and the rank of the card shows which mode is psychologically operative. The kings represent the stable, sustained and fixed mode, the queens the initiatory and instinctive cardinal mode and the knights the changeable, ambiguous and mutable mode. Thus the King of Cups corresponds to the fixed water sign Scorpio, the Queen of Pentacles is the cardinal earth sign Capricorn,

and the Knight of Wands is the mutable fire sign Sagittarius. The way we work with such images is that they signal to us that the archetype is near, whether in the guise of a person we know, a subpersonality within us of which we are not conscious, or projected onto others around us. This shows us the extent to which we have been able to recognize, identify with or integrate the subpersonality in question. For example, if our anger is aroused on a deep level we are likely to draw the King of Cups, corresponding to the sign Scorpio, which describes anger that has been buried within and sustained on deeper psychological levels.

The Page of each suit is the elemental action on the personality level. The Page of Swords is therefore the attribute of thought, the Page of

PAGE of SWORDS

ABOVE THE COURT CARDS
MAY REPRESENT CHARACTER
TYPES. FOR EXAMPLE, THE
PAGE OF SWORDS IS
INTELLECTUAL THINKING.

THE PIP CARDS

The pip cards are numbered from ace to 10 of each suit and correspond to a process of development from first manifestation to completion of the quality of the element. A typical scheme for understanding the Minor Arcana numbers is as follows:

1   The aces are the root or seed of the element.
2   The twos are the element in a pure manifest and uncontaminated way.
3   The threes are the fertilization of the element with an inherent stability.
4   The fours are a solidification and materialization of the element.
5   The fives mobilize and upset the static and stable system and bring change.
6   The sixes are most harmonized, centred and balanced.
7   The sevens are degeneration, weakness and loss of stability.
8   The eights are the unexpected shift caused by an acknowledgement of error.
9   The nines are the crystallization and full impact of the elemental energy in a material way.
10 The 10s are the end of the process and the final transformation into rigidity.

(Camphausen, Rufus, *Mind Mirror*, pp.66-8.)

Wands of intuition or energy; the Page of Pentacles of sensuality and physicality; and the Page of Cups of emotion and feeling. Their action is such that they represent the element but without a clearly defined mode of operation. They would be carried by a person who embodied thought, but who might not have specific ideas attractive to you.

The court cards are also aspects of the spiritual principle, although in many decks, including the Universal Waite deck used in this book, there is an imbalance of male and female personifications.

Typically for early decks, the male triad of King-Knight-Page was counterbalanced by the feminine influence of the Queen. In some Italian decks the knights were balanced by ladies, and in Crowley's Thoth tarot he uses princes and princesses to make two evenly balanced pairs.

THE SUIT OF WANDS

The Wands are the element Fire and the psychological function of intuition.

ACE OF WANDS – AWAKENING SPIRIT
A hand emerges from the clouds holding a wand in bloom.

ACE of WANDS.

INTERPRETATION
Beginning the quest for self; initiatory energy awaiting direction from above; creativity and invention; understanding one's family and origins; enterprising spirit; money; fortune and inheritance.

Reversed: Blind energy without direction; resisting seeing the self; decadence; a clouded joy.

TWO OF WANDS – DOMINION
A powerful man holds a globe and staff as he looks across the sea from the battlements of a castle above the tranquil countryside. To his left a cube of stone is decorated with roses and lilies in a cross.

INTERPRETATION
Power and integration bring worldly success and riches; conquest and marriage; the isolation of high position; adventure and domination.

Reversed: Sadness amidst wealth; wonder and surprise; too much independence; isolation.

THREE OF WANDS – VIRTUE

A serene personage is seen from the back, watching ships passing

from cliffs overlooking the sea. He leans upon one of the three staves growing from the ground.

INTERPRETATION

Personal strength originates with integrity; an alignment of energy and feelings brings powerful action; bringing unconscious contents to awareness leads to cooperation and success; business ventures succeed, especially when dealing with foreign countries.

Reversed: Immaturity and a failure of nerve; willpower undirected; an end of troubles through full disclosure; suspension of adversity.

FOUR OF WANDS – COMPLETION

A garland suspended from four staves frames two female figures holding bouquets of flowers. Behind them the manor house is protected by an arching bridge.

INTERPRETATION

Stability comes from completing tasks and perfecting the expression

of the self; initiative and leadership applied to proper planning lead to success and security; starting a successful venture; prosperity and peace at home; bridging the spiritual and physical worlds.

Reversed: Instability caused by short-sighted goals or a lack of clear objectives; exaggerated expectations; premature expectations; but also, increase and beauty even when reversed.

FIVE OF WANDS – STRIFE

The five of wands shows a group of five young men banging wooden staves together in an act that mimics warfare although they are doing no harm to one another.

INTERPRETATION

Anxiety and frustration are caused by an excess of energy without sufficient direction; holding back from commitment; shallow imitation; struggling for success and riches; possible gain; noble aims without the backup of authority; self-advancement.

Reversed: Artificial shows of strength or direction; emptiness and arrogance; optimism without sufficient grounds; lawsuits and trickery.

SIX OF WANDS – VICTORY

A young man on a white horse is wearing the laurel wreath of victory and bearing a staff that is also crowned with a laurel wreath. Footmen with staves walk by his side.

INTERPRETATION

Positive expectation and self-confidence bring optimism for long-term goals; expansion of awareness and openness for psychological

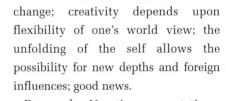

change; creativity depends upon flexibility of one's world view; the unfolding of the self allows the possibility for new depths and foreign influences; good news.

Reversed: Negative expectations; pessimism caused by difficulties opening up; closing down and suppressing the self; vanity and self-admiration.

SEVEN OF WANDS - VALOUR

A young man standing in a belligerent pose at the edge of a cliff defends himself against six aggressive staves from below.

INTERPRETATION

Standing by beliefs; the courage to resist compromise; enterprise and initiative meet with resistance requiring perseverance; the strength to protect one's own spiritual position; gaining and defending higher ground.

Reversed: Abandoning beliefs; being forced to retire from a stance; caution against indecision.

EIGHT OF WANDS - FLIGHT

A squadron of eight wands fly through the tranquil countryside. They fly towards the ground, like arrows.

INTERPRETATION

Expansive intuitions require a change of location; modifying direction; optimistically believing in the future; taking prophecies seriously; approaching a speedy end to an issue; love affairs.

Reversed: Lack of intuition brings wrong turns and a general aimlessness; excessive vanity and egotism; domestic disputes.

NINE OF WANDS - STRENGTH

An injured and forlorn, but still powerful and dominant figure leans firmly on his staff in front of a wall of staves. His aggressive appearance and stance show that he is facing attack from the east.

Being strong in opposition; facing outer challenges to inner attitudes; perception and instinct join to bring victory; strength created by overcoming physical and energetic opposition from the status quo.

Reversed: Being an outsider with unusual ideas; fleeing inner challenges; obstacles behind and in front; adversity.

10 OF WANDS – OPPRESSION

A strong man is carrying 10 heavy staves towards a small rural village.

Interpretation

Holding back creative powers or self expression through lack of energy or direction; spiritual goals compromised by physical considerations; self-limiting visions of what is possible.

Reversed: Contradictory circumstances; jumping to irrational conclusions; lawsuits with little chance of winning; intrigues.

PAGE OF WANDS – PURE INTUITION

A brave young man places his vertical sprouting wand skyward in expectation. He is dressed in gold and red, the fiery colours. His vestments are decorated with salamanders of fire.

Interpretation

The impetuosity and boundless energy of youth; energy and aspiration without direction; a provider of force; loyal friend and associate unable to take control of a situation; brilliant and daring energies; adolescent enthusiasm.

Reversed: Denying free spirit; indecision and instability; evil news.

77

KNIGHT OF WANDS – FLEXIBLE INTUITION

Astride a galloping battle horse, the extremely confident Knight of Wands charges towards his goal, passing pyramids in the distance. His tunic is decorated with elemental salamanders of fire and gold and red flames decorate his robe and helmet.

INTERPRETATION

Exciting youngsters in your life; sudden changes in life direction; expressing new and exciting philosophical and religious perceptions; intuitive messages from spiritual domains lead to a journey; adventures in consciousness; passionate creativity; flight and precipitate action.

Reversed: Disappearing without trace; loss of inspiration; psychological cul-de-sacs requiring forceful change.

QUEEN OF WANDS – INITIATORY SELF

Upon her throne of fire, decorated with lions and holding an open sunflower, the Queen of Wands faces the south, from which the sun's rays are strongest and most penetrating. The pyramids behind her and the cat at her feet symbolize the Egyptian heritage of her divine right.

INTERPRETATION

A dark, chaste and honourable woman facing life issues; Aries or fire sign people, especially women. Sureness and penetration of the open self; powerful self-assertion and awareness of direction; success in business and creative affairs.

Reversed: Lack of self-awareness or self-assertion; obstinacy and jealousy; experiencing opposition to your pure energy.

KING OF WANDS – CONSCIOUS SELF

Wearing a flowing cape, a crown of flames and a leonine medallion, the King of Wands sits upon a throne emblazoned with lions. At his feet is a salamander, the alchemical symbol for fire. He gazes towards the East where his totem the Sun rises to bring light into the day.

INTERPRETATION

A dark, honest and friendly man; Leo or fire sign people: the lion within. Self-consciousness and commitment to the quest of attaining greater awareness; spiritual vision and the need to be fixed upon the right path; loyalty and faithfulness.

Reversed: Stubbornness from fixed views incapable of change; spiritual arrogance.

THE SUIT OF CUPS

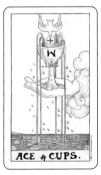

Cups are the element water and the psychological function of feeling.

ACE OF CUPS – TRUE HEART

A hand from the clouds surrounded by dew holds a cup from which four streams of water fall into a tranquil pond. A white dove descends to place a cross-marked wafer into the cup.

INTERPRETATION

The open heart is true at the beginning of the spiritual adventure; joy and contentment; abundance and fertility; expressing true feelings; openness to deep feelings; the regeneration of love. Reversed: Inability to open the heart; false heart; instability; emotional inconstancy and insensitivity.

TWO OF CUPS – LOVE

A young woman and man are exchanging cups to pledge their union. Above them a caduceus of Hermes is crowned by a lion's head.

INTERPRETATION

The interrelationship between male and female energies within; nurturing and inspired love; sympathy and concord; clarity and focus in relationship.

Reversed: Lack of nurturing; inappropriate feelings between the sexes; too much dependency.

THREE OF CUPS – ABUNDANCE

Three maidens lofting cups toast themselves and the bountiful world around them.

INTERPRETATION

Expressing emotional diversity and plenty brings abundance in the outer world; expressive relationships with equals; victory; healing energies from a group or family; deep communication and communion with others.

Reversed: Trapped emotions and buried feelings; inexpressive relationships; emotional breakdown; excessive pleasures; achievement.

FOUR OF CUPS – BLENDED PLEASURE

An unhappy, apathetic young man seated under a tree contemplates three cups before him and one held by a hand emerging from a cloud.

INTERPRETATION

Deep sensitivity to outer influences brings a need for withdrawal; devotion to higher feelings;

emotional over-expression; succumbing to seduction and pleasure; being confused by outer/inner emotional conflicts.

Reversed: New instructions and teachers; clouded reality from taking in more than one can really understand; also disappointment with luxury.

FIVE OF CUPS – EMOTIONAL DISAPPOINTMENT

A dark, cloaked figure looks down at three spilt cups with two upright cups behind him. The bridge over the river in the background leads to a small isolated castle.

INTERPRETATION

Deep disappointment despite fullness; courage and work required in a relationship; relationships that do not correspond to expectations; unsatisfactory inheritance; a bitter marriage; strong unconscious needs not met.

Reversed: Upsetting news; new alliances with old friends; projects with unknown values and uncertain goals.

SIX OF CUPS – NOSTALGIA

Two young children play in a garden with cups filled with blossoming flowers.

INTERPRETATION

Memories of blissful childhood times bring pleasure and happiness; positive reinforcement from past memories; contact and identification with the inner child; receiving supportive or parental feelings.

Reversed: Renewal; the potential for re-generation; emotional turmoil.

SEVEN OF CUPS – SENTIMENT

A dark figure observes cups filled with fantastic visionary treasures in the clouds.

INTERPRETATION

Reflections or projections of emotional states upon the ideal; attaining the insubstantial; sentimental attachments; need to balance psychic sensitivity with honesty.

Reversed: False emotional projections; being overwhelmed by desire or taken in by fantasy; projects based on will.

EIGHT OF CUPS – ABANDONMENT

A dejected man walks away from a pyramid of cups towards the mountains and the sea. The full moon gleams above.

INTERPRETATION

Abandoning one's previous feelings; retreat after being emotionally drained; the decline of a formerly fulfilling relationship; departing from family; timidity and mildness.

Reversed: Joy and happiness; returning to face difficult emotional pressures; the end of isolation.

NINE OF CUPS – SATISFACTION

An overweight man with crossed arms sits in front of a table full of wine goblets, implying plenty and abundance.

INTERPRETATION

An awareness of emotional satisfaction; material security leads to feeling secure; concord; satisfaction in an outstanding issue. Reversed:

Truth and loyalty; psychological vulnerability; openness to emotional pressure.

10 OF CUPS – CONTENTMENT

A vivid rainbow of cups arches over an ecstatic couple and their dancing children. Beyond is a beautiful homeland beyond the river.

INTERPRETATION

Emotional completion; discovering the riches in your dreams; heartfelt repose: successful artistic activity; idealistic feelings must be experienced in reality.

Reversed: False security; dreams exceed reality; indignation and egocentricity.

PAGE OF CUPS – PURE FEELING

A fair and attractive page contemplates a fish arising from his cup. Behind him the waters rise and fall.

PAGE of CUPS.

INTERPRETATION

An emotionally involved partner; studying feelings as they arise; turning fish into princesses; fantasies about potential openings; the beginning of a relationship; meditation and study.

Reversed: Emotional detachment; dreaming about fantastic relationships, and emotional dependency.

KNIGHT of CUPS.

KNIGHT OF CUPS – GRACEFUL FEELING

A beautiful and gentle knight wearing a winged helmet holds a cup towards his future as he dreams of true love.

INTERPRETATION

Approaching the emotional core of one's being; significant dreams; passive and graceful responses to emotional situations; fateful and destined relationship in mind; messengers; an advance or proposition or invitation. Reversed: Evasive emotions; false ideals; subtle tricks; duplicity.

QUEEN OF CUPS – EMOTIONAL INTEGRITY

In a seashell throne surrounded by water, a beautiful Aphrodite-like woman gazes at a magical cup and sees her dreams within.

INTERPRETATION

Emotional service and nurturing come from an unexpected source; actions inspired by dreamy feelings; devotion and happiness; enjoyment of giving support to a partner; wisdom and virtue.

Reversed: A distinguished woman not to be trusted; perversity and treachery.

KING OF CUPS – UNCONDITIONAL LOVE

A stable and severe king sits on his seashell throne in the sea. He is holding a cup and sceptre. A ship passes on one side and a dolphin on the other. He wears a fish dangling from his neck and is at home in the waves.

INTERPRETATION

A fair and emotionally secure person; emotional commitment and unconditional love; an emotional obligation is fulfilled; scientists and artists unite; creative intelligence.

Reversed: Emotional insecurity and lack of commitment; injustice; scandals due to uncontrolled feelings; losses through passion.

THE SUIT OF SWORDS

Swords are the element Air and the psychological function of thinking and mental activity.

ACE OF SWORDS – INNOVATIVE THOUGHT

A hand coming from a cloud holds a sword penetrating a crown draped with laurel leaves. There are mountains in the background.

INTERPRETATION

Communicating ideas for their own sake; invention and discrimination in thought; placing priority upon ideas; mental identification.

Reversed: Detachment and abstraction; a breakdown of communication; a lack of ideas or goals; difficulties with intimacy.

TWO OF SWORDS – BALANCE

A woman sits by the sea balancing two crossed swords on her shoulders. She is wearing a blindfold. A waxing moon appears over her left shoulder.

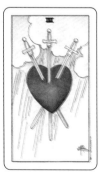

INTERPRETATION

Conforming with others' ideas; relationships with similarity of ideas and goals; meditative mind-balancing choices; affection and intimacy; friend-ship in arms.

Reversed: False ideas about others; disloyalty.

THREE OF SWORDS – SORROW

Three swords pierce a heart amidst rain clouds.

INTERPRETATION

Being influenced by past difficulties; sadness removing you from present time; difficulties in relationships due to disloyalty; delay.

Reversed: Clearing up past attitudes; investigating negative thoughts about your past.

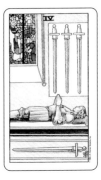

FOUR OF SWORDS – PEACE

The tomb of a knight lying in state with three swords on the wall and one on his tomb.

INTERPRETATION

Allowing destructive ideas to pass away; remembering life as sacred; exile from society; resolving conflicts through unattachment.

Reversed: Obsession with negative past influences; denying yourself rest; wise administration; economy and caution in all matters.

FIVE OF SWORDS – DEFEAT

A man carrying three swords has just vanquished two foes in battle. He possesses the field as they walk away in defeat.

INTERPRETATION

The defeat and destruction of a negative behaviour pattern; lack of integration of subpersonalities; destruction of existing ideas; loss and dishonour.

Reversed: Unreliability because of unpredictable ideas; not accepting obsolete ideas.

SIX OF SWORDS – PROGRESSIVE MIND

A ferryman punts two hooded passengers across a river. Six vertical swords stand in the front of the boat.

Progressive ideas require unusual means of communication; integrating ideas; separation due to inventiveness; eccentricity of thought; a journey by water; acting as an emissary.

Reversed: Ideas not accepted as being too inventive; lack of originality; confessions.

SEVEN OF SWORDS – FUTILITY

Before a tournament tent a man carries off five swords, but leaves two behind in the ground.

INTERPRETATION

Taking on too many new ideas; unconventional and individual attitudes provoke ostracism; plans that may fail; unrealistic designs; competition without resolution.

Reversed: Eccentric attitudes; good advice and counsel; instructing others; uncertainty.

EIGHT OF SWORDS – INTERFERENCE

A bound and masked woman stands amidst a field of swords.

INTERPRETATION

Being trapped by obsolete ideas or mental concepts; blindness to one's own communications; overly analytical; mental originality without proper focussing.

Reversed: Disquiet; being trapped by design; opposition; unforeseen difficulties; too much complexity.

NINE OF SWORDS – DECEPTION

A weeping woman sits up in her bed decorated with zodiacal symbols, underneath a wall of horizontal swords.

INTERPRETATION

Desolation caused by negative thinking; failure of a plan of action; disappointment from excessive criticism of the self.

Reversed: Being trapped in negative thought patterns; suspicion caused within oneself; fears supported by others; inconsistent ideas.

10 OF SWORDS – RUIN

A prostrate figure lies on the ground, pierced in the back by 10 swords.

INTERPRETATION

Afflicted by negative ideas; the death of a concept or life direction; contradictory information kills communication; lies and sadness.

Reversed: Advantages and profit; the break-down of authority.

PAGE OF SWORDS – PURE THINKING

A figure ready for action holds an upright sword amidst rough countryside.

INTERPRETATION

Bringing ideas into the physical world; mental identification; the need to examine thoughts; logic and organizational enterprises; secrecy and hidden communications.

Reversed: Resistance to thinking; being unaware of your ideas; the unforeseen; sickness.

KNIGHT OF SWORDS – CREATIVE THINKING

The brave and romantic hero charges, scattering all his enemies before him.

INTERPRETATION

Inspiration that is not bound by any constructs; free-ranging mind; cleverness and skill at self-expression and communication; verbal jousting and competition; changes and versatility.

Reversed: Constrained by attitude; limited intelligence; superficial ideas and skills; shallow thought.

QUEEN OF SWORDS – PERCEPTIVE THINKING

A regal woman raises a vertical sword and extends her left hand in a gesture of acknowledgment.

INTERPRETATION

Balanced feminine thinking and communication; integration of thoughts and personality; a peace-maker or mediator; partnership with others and the world; chastity.

Reversed: Psychological imbalance weighted toward the feminine; a vindictive woman; feelings of malice.

89

KING OF SWORDS – JUDGMENTAL THINKING

A stern ruler sits in judgment holding a sword of discrimination vertically.

INTERPRETATION

The discriminative male principle; balanced masculine thinking and judgment; an arbitrator or advocate; power and command of the mind; authority; strategic thinking.

Reversed: Lacking discrimination with blatant favouritism; imbalanced male thinking; judgmental attitudes; cruelty and perversity.

THE SUIT OF PENTACLES

Pentacles are the element Earth and the psychological function of sensation.

ACE OF PENTACLES – CONTENTMENT
A hand extending from the clouds holds a pentacle above a beautiful enclosed garden.

INTERPRETATION

Balance between body and higher functions of mind, spirit and feelings; ecstasy; inheritance of earthly power and possessions; good health and abundance.

Reversed: Imbalance between higher functions and physical reality; illness; abandoning or losing possessions.

TWO OF PENTACLES – CHANGE
A dancing young man holds pentacles in each hand, joined by an endless cord making a lemniscate, a symbol of infinity.

INTERPRETATION

Understanding cycles of birth, death and rebirth in the physical world; expanding awareness through change; recognizing the idea of polarity in life; agitation and duality.

Reversed: Anxiety caused by limited views; being trapped on the wheel of rebirth; life as a grind; futility and simulated enjoyment.

THREE OF PENTACLES – SKILLFUL ACTION
A mason or sculptor rebuilds an archway in sight of two monks.

INTERPRETATION

Understanding artistic priorities in creating a bridge of understanding; taking control of a project or stage of development;

rebuilding the structure; mobility and arist-ocracy.

Reversed: Purely mechanical actions; allowing bridges to break down; indolence and pettiness; weakness.

FOUR OF PENTACLES – POWER

A crowned man, wearing a pentacle crown, rotates a pentacle in his

arms. Two more pentacles can be seen firmly placed underneath his feet. There is a large city in the background.

INTERPRETATION

Awareness of boundaries brings power and possessions; practical and realistic methods for attaining physical security; defining oneself by possessions or wealth; thinking about the real world.

Reversed: Possessiveness; unclear boundaries; inability to put limits on oneself.

FIVE OF PENTACLES – POVERTY

Two injured and poor people pass under stained-glass window, which is decorated with five pentacles, during a snowstorm.

INTERPRETATION

Material insecurity caused by misunderstanding the physical world; unusual priorities; abusing or ignoring the body; letting go of worry about financial matters; release.

Reversed: Disorder and chaos from abandon-ing the world order; the breakdown of physical structures; strain, discord and ruin.

SIX OF PENTACLES – SUCCESS

A successful, rich and sensitive merchant bestows money on the poor and needy.

INTERPRETATION

Harmonious representation of the earthly element; positive sensations, gifts and gratification; present prosperity and success in worldly affairs, but eventual change.

Reversed: Desire and materialistic attitudes; physical changes requiring penitence.

SEVEN OF PENTACLES – ANXIETY

A worried young man leans on his staff and observes the fruits of his labour

INTERPRETATION

Fear of satisfaction or completion; limitations in productivity; recognizing barriers; the need for exchange; the harvest means the end of a project or endeavour.

Reversed: Inability to complete; resistance to physical requirements; anxiety regarding financial commitments.

EIGHT OF PENTACLES – CRAFT

An artist carves pentacles for trophies.

INTERPRETATION

Attending to details in one's work or creative efforts; skill in material matters; successful planning for the future; knowledge of the workings of the world.

Reversed: Avoiding the details; material ignorance; difficulties in saving.

NINE OF PENTACLES – ACCOMPLISHMENT

A beautiful woman stands alone amidst a splendid garden of great abundance and fruitfulness. There is a hooded hunting falcon on her wrist.

INTERPRETATION

Awareness of realistic goals; bringing desires and needs into line; adjusting goals to allow satisfaction; good luck and good management.

Reversed: Unrealistic expectations in the physical world; being governed by base instincts; bad faith.

10 OF PENTACLES – WEALTH

A woman and man, accompanied by their child, converse beneath an archway that leads to a manor house. Two white dogs look curiously at an old grey-haired man who is in front of the doorway.

93

INTERPRETATION

Protecting the security of the family and home; the family system of generations; a loving environment; a final abode.

Reversed: Breakdown of the family system; lack of understanding between generations; misusing past memories.

PAGE OF PENTACLES – PURE FORM

A youthful gentleman meditates on the pentacle he is holding in his raised hands, ignoring the countryside around him. A sacred grove awaits him on a distant hillside.

INTERPRETATION

The stage just before transformation; meditation on strength and beauty; approaching spiritual work; application and studying; reflection upon material and spiritual goals.

Reversed: Resisting transformation; being unable to detach and obtain objectivity; dissipating spiritual possibilities; unfavourable news.

KNIGHT OF PENTACLES – CREATED FORM

A solid and secure horseman holds a pentacle, but looks beyond it to the distant horizon.

INTERPRETATION

Great energy applied to basic and solid tasks; long-term expectations and goals; attention to physical details; responsibility and service as a profession.

Reversed: Lack of inspiration; inability to deal with present situations; too much emphasis upon stability.

QUEEN OF PENTACLES – NURTURING FORM

A dark and introspective woman protects the pentacle she holds on her lap. Her throne stands amidst a wonderful arbor as she meditates upon the plight of the soul.

INTERPRETATION

Searching for the inner meaning of the physical world; correcting priorities; feminine intelligence and introspection; a great soul; seeing all elements within the physical.

Reversed: Suspicion caused by materialism; ambition and detachment.

KING OF PENTACLES

KING OF PENTACLES – SKILLFUL FORM

A dark man sits upon a throne decorated with bulls' heads in great solidity and security. Behind the throne a prosperous city stands.

INTERPRETATION

Manifesting skill in the physical world; the ability to build and sustain; realizing intelligence; aptitude for business and attain-ments in the material sphere; fixed concerns.

Reversed: Victimized by materialism; being arrogant due to wealth; being trapped by physical trappings.

THE MAGICIAN

THE TAROT READING

CHAPTER SIX

Reading the tarot cards is divination, a ritual or ceremonial act, a magical action and a meditation. Divination means 'from the divine', and implies that communication with higher intelligence or beings is sought, although within the psychological context this may be understood as higher aspects of one's self, higher levels of consciousness or positive subpersonalities.

In divination, a question is posed and the answer determined by interpreting patterns created in the natural world or by a personal and conscious act, as in the case of laying out tarot cards. In ancient

ABOVE READING THE TAROT CARDS IS A MYSTICAL ACT THAT REVEALS HIDDEN MESSAGES AND ALLOWS US TO COMMUNICATE WITH OUR UNCONSCIOUS SELF.

times divination took a multitude of forms. The movement of birds across the sky, the form and colour of the entrails of animals, the patterns of bones thrown onto the ground, the numbers of groups of sticks divided and counted were the raw material of these mantic arts. In each case a vocabulary of symbolic patterns or shapes determined an answer to the question. The diviner interpreted the oracular response and, as such, became a direct conduit, or channel, to the gods or goddesses. We can look back in history and find the importance of oracular centres such as Delphi, Thebes, Glastonbury, Tara, Babylon, Sidon and others spread across

Europe and Asia. In many cultures such contact with the divine was encouraged as a central belief, if not the core, of religious observance. Today we seek the gods or goddesses within ourselves.

But how do oracles work? The psychologist Carl Jung studied these phenomena for many decades, and indeed wrote a famous foreword to the translation of the *I Ching* by Richard Wilhelm. Jung postulated that there is a 'synchronicity' between outer events and inner psychic states, which means that outer and inner influences are linked by similar meaning, and that there is no such thing as coincidence. Every event in the universe is connected in some way with every other event, if only the connection can be known. Any technique for tapping into the temporal flow, whether it be the I Ching or tarot cards, allows access to this fount of information and understanding.

Tarot taps into the information available in the space-time continuum at a specific time and place. The symbols of the tarot are the receivers, as it were, of this information. They are mirrors of the self, both in the sense that they reflect the state of awareness of certain issues, and that they provide many layers of meaning that will be decoded according to the openness and symbol-reading abilities of the querent.

THE QUESTION AND THE QUERENT

The practice of tarot brings the realization that if the true nature of the question were understood, that itself would constitute the answer. In practice, the way in which a question is asked often betrays the answer, as though the answer is in some mysterious way hidden within the question. Similarly, using tarot makes us aware that the answers lie within the images, simply awaiting our recognition of them.

The formulation of the question has the primary function of focusing the mind upon the self and its true issues. It is often the case that the more precise the question, the more preordained the answer. It is therefore important that the quality of the question is directly related to the quality of the answer. When a question is clearly expressed, the answer is usually not far away.

When a question involves another person or outer circumstances apparently beyond the querent's control, one must immediately recognize that an issue of projection is central to the answer. Why is the outside world affecting this person in such a complete way? A request for a more tightly formulated question will often give rise to resistances and breakthroughs that will initiate an inward-looking process. The inclusion of the querent brings the question to life. The more personal the question, the closer to home the entire process.

A valuable exercise is to ask yourself to formulate a question that is critical to you right now. As you try to formulate the question, feel and observe what goes on inside, what territory your mind covers on its way to discovering the question. Often you will review possible answers while formulating the questions, or experience blocks to asking certain ones. In a tarot reading, the chances are that the cards will symbolize this process.

In some situations, the querent does not have a specific question. Many first-time tarot querents ask – 'What is going to happen to me in the future?' In this case the mere act of contemplating possible questions will at least focus the mind and concentrate the attention upon the present time.

INTERPRETING A READING

RIGHT BEFORE YOU HAVE A READING, THINK CAREFULLY ABOUT THE QUESTION YOU ARE GOING TO ASK OF THE CARDS. THE QUALITY OF THE ANSWER WILL DEPEND ON THE QUALITY OF THE QUESTION.

THE RITUAL OF TAROT

The main objective of the preliminaries to the ritual of tarot is to allow the querent and reader to relax, to quieten the mind and to concentrate upon the issues at hand. If the process is to be important for you, it is recommended you follow all or some of the following guidelines:

1 Create as controlled an environment as you can; determine the time of play when your concentration will be best, and you are least likely to be disturbed.

2 The energy of the cards should not be diluted by contact with others or with impure surroundings, so many tarot readers keep their deck wrapped in a silk cloth or a box, hidden from view. It is also useful to have a special sheet of silk or cloth upon which to read the cards.

3 Turn out the light. Light some candles. Burn incense.

4 Wear comfortable and loose clothing. It may also be desirable to meditate before approaching the cards.

5 Recite an invocation or one of the affirmations to create the correct atmosphere for the reading. You may want to have ritual elements available – a cup of wine, a sword, a wand and a pentacle or coin – to intensify the mood.

6 It is important that the two individuals involved in the process are psychically linked – make eye contact, attempt to join energies in the process ahead.

7 Keep a diary or book in which to write down tarot readings. You will enjoy, and learn about, tarot by keeping such records.

99

How does one arrive at accurate conclusions from the cards? The answer is, predictably, quite complex. There are many issues at stake in converting a card in a tarot spread to a sensible interpretation that can be understood by a client. What is obvious is that the interpretation must be a combination of:

- *The traditional interpretative meanings of the cards.*
- *Images or ideas derived from the symbols on the cards.*
- *A feeling or intuitive response to the individual querent and her or his question.*

The interpretative meanings given in this book are intended only as a guide to possible directions implied by each card, rather than literal interpretations, but beginners may be tempted to look at the card in a spread, turn to the appropriate page of this or another book, and read the interpretation that seems most relevant to the client. With experience, and practice, a tarot reader will learn and remember the meanings associated with each card and store this information for easy access. But, an encyclopedic memory of traditional interpretations will not make one a superior tarot reader. This requires the use of intuition, feeling and compassion for the client and his or her plight, and the ability to derive from the symbols upon the cards the higher meanings needed.

The interpretation of the symbols on tarot cards is a process similar to interpreting dreams. In both cases the images must be seen as metaphors for unconscious principles of the dreamer/client. The personae of the cards are aspects of the client's personality; their environments are moods or attitudes of the client; the symbols of the cards are psychic mechanisms or tools that the individual may choose to use. Thus, the sword sticking into a prone body can be seen as an important idea (swords are the thinking process and ideas) penetrating an individual who has given up hope (the prone position). Trees will imply the growth of whatever they protect and, if in the distance, show that there is growth in the future.

As in dream interpretation, it is not necessary to interpret every symbol on every card, but to meditate upon the cards and talk about what you happen to focus upon. It is natural to see a card one way today, and very differently tomorrow. In every situation the appropriate images will 'pop out' at you. The more you trust your intuition and try to put yourself in the place of your client, the more accurate and appropriate the images that present themselves will be.

As in dreams, there may not be an obvious time sequence, but rather a jumble of images apparently thrown together at random. One of your tasks is to take the multitude of images and apply a sequence to them. This process may be obvious. The Fool followed by Judgement would imply naivety leading to the necessity to make a choice, while the other way around would show that choices lead to naive actions. It is said that dream images have no sequence when they are dreamed, but that our conscious mind imposes a structure upon them at the instant we awake. In tarot interpretation we intend to do the same thing.

The position of the card should influence the way you interpret it. For cards in 'conscious' positions at the top of a spread for example, be as conscious as you can in rationally finding a meaning for the cards. For cards in 'unconscious' positions at the foot of a spread, be as free and unstructured as possible in intuitively deriving an appropriate meaning. In time you will learn to allow your mind, feelings and intuition to work together, and to blend these seemingly different functions together in a coherent whole.

The client also participates in the reading by their presence. Look at them closely as they enter the room, sit down, listen to you, take the cards, shuffle them and respond to the interpretation. Search especially for unconscious signals that the client may be sending out. Their resistance to certain cards will show you the cards represent important principles that they are blocking. If they project qualities onto their partners, friends or on you, these qualities have been difficult to integrate and need to be identified and followed up by you. Pay attention to the images they relate to or don't relate to, notice their changing posture and attention throughout the consultation. The more clues you have to work with, the more full and complete the atmosphere and the more accurate the reading.

Compare the interpretations given in the book with your own intuitively derived ideas, and modify them by the position of the card (for example, is the card in the conscious or the unconscious position?).With practice, the dedication to learn the key words and the willingness to act and talk about feelings and intuitions, you will be able to provide stimulating, challenging and accurate interpretations to your friends and clients.

LEARNING ABOUT THE CARDS

Before looking at some different tarot spreads, it is important to develop a technique for learning about the individual cards. Rather than learning the meaning of each card by rote, it is often better to try to understand the language of the symbols so that you can reconstruct and reinvent the meanings each time you use the cards. Like interpreting dreams, it is more important that you learn to develop an ability to associate freely with the cards than it is to know their literal meanings, which, in any event, are far from agreed.

THE DAILY CARD

One of the best ways to learn the tarot is to first take the 22 Major Arcana cards, isolate them from the rest of the deck, and place them in a prominent position in your home, where you can see them every day, particularly at the beginning and end of the day.

The Daily Card technique involves choosing a card every morning. When you rise, shuffle the cards, cut them, and when you have placed them down on a table, turn over the top card. This card will be your Significator, your card for the day.

Look at the card, and try to find one or more symbols that inspire you. See the colours and textures represented on the card, and try to enhance their reality in your mind. Allow the environment of the card to permeate you, to become part of you, or you a part of it. Sometimes you will express the card's meaning yourself, while often it will be acted out by others around you.

This may correlate with whether the card is upright or reversed. If you feel a resistance to the images or personifications or actions on the cards, try to understand what you are resisting, and why. If the card bores you or makes you uneasy, explore those feelings and the questions and situations that bring them up.

ABOVE BEFORE CHOOSING YOUR CARD FOR THE DAY, SHUFFLE THE CARDS THOROUGHLY. THEN CUT THE CARDS AND PLACE THEM ON THE TABLE. THE TOP CARD WILL BE YOUR SIGNIFICATOR.

Feel what it must be like to be the individual represented on the card. Put yourself in their place, whether female or male, adult or child, and imagine being that person or expressing that quality in yourself. In the case of animal representations, identify with the animal within yourself.

When you have exhausted the images in the card and are confident that you have experienced it fully, look in this book and read the text associated with the card. Read the Guided Imagery (*see* pp.26–64) and allow it to sink in, and open yourself up to the journey it describes. When you have finished, read the Affirmation (*see* pp.26–64), and if you cannot learn it on the spot, write it down on a slip of paper and repeat it throughout the day.

Think of the card's qualities as a part of you throughout the day. When you draw the Fool, go through a day where you allow yourself

THE FOOL.

ABOVE THE FOOL BEGINS AND ENDS
OUR LIFE JOURNEY – WE MUST ALLOW
OUR PURE INNER BEING TO MANIFEST
THROUGH EXPERIENCE.

to be young again, be naive, take chances or explore areas to which you never usually give attention. Try to understand why the card pictures the scene it does and how it could be relevant to you.

At the end of the day, review what has happened throughout the day. Which part of you was dominant, which part was passive? Did you feel integrated or fragmented? Was the card a useful guide or a straitjacket? Was your intuition more prominent than usual? Did you respect your inner attitudes? All these questions and their answers are valuable feedback, not only for your process of learning the cards, but also your own psychological development.

After you have become familiar with the Major Arcana cards, you may want to include the court cards and the Minor Arcana in your Daily Card reading.

THE MAGICIAN

HOW TO LAY OUT
THE CARDS

CHAPTER SEVEN

Laying out the cards is a ritualistic process, an invocation to the powers and an opening of the unconscious energies of both the reader and the querent that can be encouraged by the correct laying out of the cards. The different ways of laying out the cards are discussed in this chapter, but all begin in the following way:

1   Ask the querent hold the cards before the process begins. It is vital to be comfortable and to realize that energy must be transmitted to the cards in order for the process to work at maximum efficiency. Ask the querent to take a few minutes to meditate on the question, and then to formulate it exactly in his or her mind. Gather your mental and intuitive powers and begin the procedure.

2   When the querent is ready with a question, ask him or her to lay the deck face-down on the table and prepare to cut the cards. The deck should be cut approximately in half and then put together again. This same process can be repeated twice.

3   Each card will be taken from the top of the deck in turn and laid out in the same way. Whether they are turned from top to bottom, or from right to left, just ensure that you turn them the same way each time. If the first card is reversed, turn the entire deck around and continue placing the cards. How many cards are taken, and how they are laid out, depends on which spread has been chosen.

THE PAST-PRESENT-FUTURE SPREAD

One of the most effective of the simpler spreads is the Past-Present-Future Spread, which uses four cards. The sequence in which the cards are laid down is:

1   The Significator (Present Time)
2   The Crossing (challenges Present) – laid across the Significator
3   The Past – laid to the left of the Significator and Crossing
4   The Future – laid to the right of the Significator and Crossing

This spread shows cards symbolizing the past of the event (its causes), the present circumstances and challenges and its outcome. This spread may be applied to an event, a decision to be made or a psychological process that requires thought and action.

Shuffle the cards carefully. Then make sure that half the deck is reversed by taking the cards, cutting them and laying them down on the table as two stacks. Turn one of the stacks upside down.

The pack that remains upright is your conscious mind, while the reversed pack is your unconscious mind. Shuffle them together to integrate alchemically your conscious and unconscious, and then begin the spread.

This sample interpretation to a question will illustrate the process of stating and understanding the spread.

QUESTION:
What is the significance of my meeting today with John Smith?

THE ANSWER:
1   The Significator = Wheel of Fortune (upright)
At the present time you are aware that you are open to taking chances with relationships and exploring your abilities to open up to others, whatever their beliefs. You are inclined to take risks with your ideas and understanding of others, and so are likely to be fortunate in this relationship, which will provide you with opportunities to develop.

THE CHALLENGE OF THE CROSSING CARD

In traditional tarot lore, the central card in a reading functions as a focus of the question, as a significator of the querent or the present time, and as the potential catalyst for the issue or issues contained in the question. It is simultaneously the starting point and also the answer to the question. This implies that the answer lies within the question, similarly to the way in which the resolution of any psychological issue lies within the individual psyche.

The Crossing card is placed across the Significator or central card and symbolizes the challenge to the question and querent. It symbolizes the energy that blocks the principle shown by the Significator and simultaneously shows the bridge over which the querent must pass in order to resolve the issue and achieve wholeness. This is one reason why each of 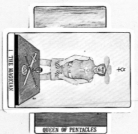 the Major Arcana cards may be understood as having both conscious and unconscious interpretations. The unconscious is usually associated with the negative because of its identity with the shadow, which has always been seen as mysterious, threatening and destructive. We fear and avoid our own negative sides, yet integration requires probing these depths, bringing their contents up into consciousness, and utilizing them as necessary parts of our whole being. This is why the Crossing card has such power and importance, and why virtually all tarot spreads utilize this combination of two cards in its centre. We need to explore the crossing card in greater detail and with more insight than the other cards, particularly if it is reversed. In a way, all other cards represent a fragmentation of the central issue of self and shadow.

2 The Crossing = The Lovers (reversed)

You are unlikely to be aware of the implications of the relationship you are initiating with this individual, particularly because you value the process over the outcome. In accepting whatever relationships come along, you are undervaluing yourself and lessening your self worth. By exerting more discrimination and control, you will create a higher awareness within yourself (and others), rather than be prone to infatuations or brotherly-sisterly communications that are not equal and challenging for you.

3 The Past = The Fool (upright)

You are conscious that in the past you have been enthusiastic and spontaneous in your response to new people in your life, without considering your own needs or understanding the implications of the relationship. You have either accepted them completely or rejected their company, without allowing a negotiation between you. As a result, your ability to make appropriate relationships has been unpredictable and unsure.

4 The Future = The Star (reversed)

Although you may not be aware of it, you are entering a relationship that will force you to take responsibility for yourself, will access deep areas and reverse life-long patterns. You are being led into a process of change that has been experienced by many, and in some ways are responding to collective impulses rather than personal ones. In order to attain fulfilment in this relationship you must be more conscious of who you are and how you relate to others.

Because the first two cards were upright and the last two reversed, the querent would be expected to move from areas in which he/she is conscious to a relationship that is increasingly unconscious, yet taps and utilizes deeper levels of their self-awareness. Such a trend is important to identify, and the movement from the Fool to the Star does follow the natural evolution of tarot itself, from naivety to a recognition of one's own worth through changing life patterns. In this sense the reading may initiate and aid further and deeper understanding of life motives.

This spread is helpful for obtaining feedback about decisions or actions to be undertaken, or for providing directions in navigating through personal, psychological processes.

THE CELTIC CROSS SPREAD

The Celtic Cross is a classic spread, known to have been used since the Middle Ages. Its function is to show a range of possibilities at a given moment, although a more modern way of interpreting the spread is to discover the level of awareness and the conditions acting upon a querent. The spread utilizes the cross shape and also four further cards in a vertical line.

The traditional Celtic Cross spread is often done with Major Arcana cards only. Therefore separate out the 21 Major Arcana cards and place them in numerical order on the table before the querent. Have the querent shuffle the cards while thinking about the question, and then state the question.

Upon stating the question, have the querent place the cards down in the following sequence:

1st   Present Position – in the middle. Represents the present situation and circumstances of the querent.

2nd   Immediate Influences – crosses the first card. Shows the domain of the question and the blockages and obstacles to be anticipated.

3rd   Destiny – above first card. The goals and ultimate destiny.

4th   Foundation – to the right of the first card. Basic influences that existed in the past as a foundation of the question.

5th   Recent Past – below the first card. Influences that are passing or have just passed through the life of the querent.

6th   Future – to the left of the first card. Where the question will lead the querent.

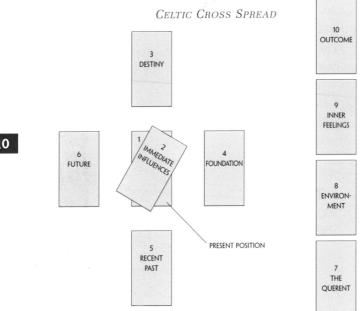

CELTIC CROSS SPREAD

Then, in a vertical line beginning at the bottom:

7th   The querent – at the bottom. Present situation and presenting issues of the querent.

8th   Environment – second up. The influence of the querent on others and their influence upon the querent.

9th   Inner Feelings – third up. The hopes, fears and inner feelings as well as secrets of the querent.

10th Outcome – at the top. The outcome that results from the previous nine cards.

In the interpretation, the reader will discover relationships between cards or positions that allow the querent to make connections that may not be obvious to him or her. Some cards will be particularly interesting to the querent, and not others. This may indicate areas in which the querent would be well advised to study his or her actions and implications more fully. There may, for example, be a connection between the immediate influences and the recent past. Cards in the spread that are reversed will indicate areas in which the querent is likely to be unaware or unconscious of his or her actions and need further attention.

111

THE ASTROLOGICAL SPREAD

This spread is called the Astrological Spread because it utilizes 12 cards around the significator, which correspond to the signs or houses of astrology. The starting point of this spread is the card to the left, the Ascendant, where the sun rises in the morning in the east. From the Ascendant you proceed in a counter-clockwise direction around the circle.

ABOVE CARDS DRAWN IN THE CELTIC CROSS SPREAD MAY INDICATE THE AREAS OF YOUR LIFE THAT NEED PARTICULAR ATTENTION PAID TO THEM.

The great virtue of this spread is that you can apply it to virtually any time period and therefore interpret a process that will take place or has taken place. Each card around the circle can signify a period of time. If each card represents one month, the spread can describe one year of 12 months. It can also describe 12 hours, 24 hours (2 hours each), 12 days, 12 weeks, 2 years (2 months each), etc. It is obviously easier if the time period is divisible by 12, although any time period could be used.

The implication is that the spread shows a development of the question or individual through a particular time period. The spread can be used as feedback for the process of psychological or spiritual development, as a predictive tool or as a matrix for answering particular concerns of the querent.

The positions in the Astrological Spread are as follows:

1st House – Ascendant – Aries. The personality and its issues; physical appearances; self-assertion; the ability to bond with oneself or others.

2nd House – Taurus. Self-valuation; acceptance of the tangible world; physical reality and the body; money and possessions.

3rd House – Gemini. Communication; the instinctive and unconscious mind; initial education; self-expression and variety; flexibility; short journeys; relationships with brothers and sisters.

4th House – Cancer. The family system and environment; parents and their emotional values; early environment; wants and needs; feelings of kinship and belonging; identity and roots.

5th House – Leo. Exteriorizing the self; primary education; relationships with teachers; games and game playing; acting; the arts, leisure and sport; consciousness of self.

6th House – Virgo. Practical service; the health; puberty and early relationships; discrimination and distillation of experience; work attitudes and relations; making life choices.

7th House – Libra. Relationships; sublimating the self in others or the world; needs and functions of relationships; emotional, business and marital relationships; relations with the world; diplomacy.

8th House – Scorpio. The process of life and death; sexuality and conception; the metaphysical; reincarnation and past lives; others' money, feelings, ideas and energies; business affairs; magic.

9th House – Sagittarius. Religion, psychology and philosophy of life; higher union and mind; beliefs; foreign journeys; legal matters and the law; athletics.

10th House – Capricorn. Ego consciousness; identification with goals and objectives in life; higher aspirations; career and occupation; parents; selfishness; pragmatism and practicality.

11th House – Aquarius. Selfless love; integration with groups or organizations; New Age concepts; sense of community; creativity and communication of ideas; social ambitions and aims; politics.

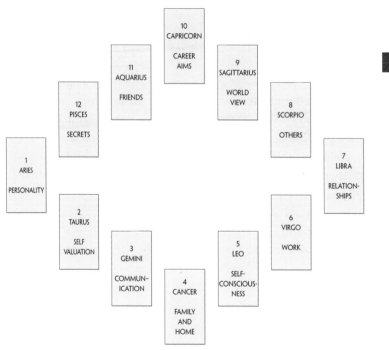

ASTROLOGICAL SPREAD

CREATE YOUR OWN SPREAD

The spreads shown in this chapter demonstrate the basic principles of tarot, but it will, I hope, be clear that the cards may also be used in other original and unique ways. You can construct any set of values about which you wish for feedback and utilize the tarot to discover clues or images that will aid you in the process of self-discovery.

12th House – Pisces. Dissolution and inner perception; isolation and loneliness; spiritual service and sacrifice; seclusion and privacy; institutions and large organizations; secrets.

In using the Astrological Spread, it is possible to use selectively certain houses/signs that refer to specific questions or issues raised, or to describe an entire sequence of influences.

Once again, the Major Arcana cards will identify areas of primary importance and archetypal activity; the court cards will show particular individuals who will affect or bring certain personality issues to the fore; and the Minor Arcana cards will describe more mundane events that happen in specific areas or at certain times. The combination of cards yields a rich tapestry that can be interpreted psychologically or as a fund of information.

The Astrological Spread can also be done with the first six cards of the Celtic Cross Spread within its centre, allowing the combination of a time period with general concerns about one's spiritual orientation within it.

TAROT AND SELF-DEVELOPMENT

While the tarot cards picture kings, queens, magicians, maidens and knights, all the images are symbolic of the self and represent stages of its process of coming into being. We are constantly developing our individuality and making our potentials actual, and the actions depicted in the cards are parts of our own process crystallized in symbols. We are looking to align ourselves with a meaning in our lives, and the interpretation of the cards may shed light on the deeper mechanisms our quest embodies. We must learn to value each part of ourselves and all those around us, as well as under-stand our inner needs and aspirations, so that we may determine and maintain the correct priorities. The tarot cards may point us towards areas we over- or undervalue in our lives.

The life process is difficult at best, but nonetherless we must learn to balance its inherent seriousness against the need to play, to enjoy ourselves, our relationships and the world around us. The importance of learning when to concentrate and when to relax and forget, when to burrow into crisis and when to detach from outer events —

ABOVE THE CHARACTERS AND ACTIONS DEPICTED IN THE CARDS ARE REPRESENTA-TIVE OF OUR STATE OF BEING AND THE EVENTS IN OUR LIVES.

all these phases and rhythms of life must be understood as being integral parts of the whole. Tarot is capable of giving us some indication of these rhythms, their nature and their timings.

We all look to the future, with both positive expectations and a sense of dread. Our anticipation and the way in which we approach the future is a primary factor in the way we live our lives, and understanding the tarot involves experimenting with the many possible futures we each carry. The divinatory capabilities of the tarot therefore interact with its psychotherapeutic qualities to create dynamic visions of our future.

At the last, we are all very different individuals, with needs and expectations unique to each of us. While we may seek friendship and evaluation from our family, friends and counsellors, the ultimate responsibility for our lives rests with us. We must therefore accept the great diversity of viewpoints we carry, and work and play with our journey in our own unique way. It is important to not only study tarot, but to learn it, make it a tool for your own understanding of yourself and become your own guide in the process of being.

Our thoughts define us to an extent that we rarely recognize. When we are in a bad mood our entire life and its directions seem invalid, but when we are positive and creative our life seems extremely pleasant and we look forward to each new day. Experimentation shows that we can modify and support our mental definition of ourselves in three similar ways – meditation, creative visualization and affirmation.

MEDITATION

The tarot cards are perfectly suited as subjects for meditation because they contain imagery that supports the archetypes you may wish to explore. By spending time looking at a particular card, soaking up its details, feeling the intensity of the colours, seeing the interactions of the shapes, trying to understand and respond to the ideas behind the images, we can bring these same qualities into our own life. At times when we are depressed or lack direction it can be very helpful to meditate on a card that has the strength or direction we lack.

It is natural while meditating to be tempted to go off the track, to see and feel things that are beyond the card you are using as an embarkation point. When this happens, recognize what it is that brings you off centre, how it makes you feel, identify where it comes from and bring your mind back to the original subject. By maintaining concentration we are eventually able to identify more and more deeply with the intention of the card.

As an exercise, meditate on one card of the tarot each day for 10 minutes. Reflect on the qualities that the card possesses, and also upon the feelings, thoughts, spiritual insights and sensations that accompany your meditation. They will provide you with clues that will lead to further development of your self. When you reach a point

ABOVE CONCENTRATE

YOUR THOUGHTS ON A SINGLE CARD. THIS WILL

HELP YOU TO UNDERSTAND BOTH THE CARD AND

YOURSELF MORE FULLY.

117

where you feel the content is uninteresting or you get bored with the imagery, that is a signal that you are coming into contact with deeper levels of your own being and should proceed beyond and push through your resistances. Insights into your life and your self often come at the point when you are experiencing the greatest resistance.

Familiarity with the tarot cards will tap you into a deep stream of knowledge and understanding that you will find refreshing and stimulating. After some time you will begin to understand the higher implications of the images, the transpersonal levels that lie beyond your normal state.

CREATIVE VISUALIZATION

ABOVE BY VISUALIZING THE IMAGES OF THE TAROT CARDS AND REFLECTING UPON THEM, WE LEARN TO IDENTIFY WITH THE CARDS AND THE ARCHETYPES THEY REPRESENT.

Visualization helps concentration and also provides a way for us to influence our will, our ability to bring our self to awareness. If we have a friend quietly speak the guided imagery for one of the tarot cards while we are relaxed and with our eyes closed, we can enter into the experience of the tarot, feel its colours, imagine its landscapes, bring the qualities carried by the card into our lives in a real way. We can allow our self to enter into the world of the card, to surrender to its environment and its atmosphere.

With practice it becomes easier and easier to be receptive to the images of the cards, to let them dwell in our minds, and even to reflect upon them when we are not looking at them. Through time we learn to identify with the cards, with the archetypal states they represent, and therefore bring our natural intuition to the fore and stimulate our basic creativity.

When we visualize climbing up a steep mountain, it supports our abilities to ascend in consciousness. To dive down into a deep pool of water reinforces our ability to penetrate our deepest feelings and bring back their valuable contents. When we walk through a bright and summery meadow in our visualization, we feel the warmth, and feel better psychologically. By using the cards in this way it is possible to extend your range of feelings, ideas and spiritual perceptions dramatically.

AFFIRMATIONS

Once we have identified the qualities of one of the Major Arcana cards that we wish to more actively bring into our life, we can use the affirmation associated with the card. The use of an affirmation can go beyond simply willing a change to come into being. The affirmation is an active matrix of commands made to our inner self, repeated regularly, and reinforced repeatedly. The strength of the affirmation, its language and its concepts, will determine how powerful its effect upon you will be.

The potency of an affirmation depends upon how seriously you take it. It must become an article of your faith that the principle expressed is valuable, indeed essential for you to have in your life. It is an adventure, but one that you can benefit from if you are able to bring your will into line with the potency of the affirmation. Like using creative visualization with tarot, you may experience resistance or a kind of backlash from your affirmation, but this often is a signal that the affirmation and its underlying energy are being taken in.

TAKING THE
TAROT FURTHER

CHAPTER NINE

Probably the most valuable way to increase your understanding and familiarity with the tarot is to keep a dedicated psychological work book for use with the tarot. It has been shown in modern psychotherapy that keeping a work book or diary to monitor your progress is an important way to record the workings of your inner life, your unfolding awareness of who you are and a guide to the way in which your journey develops.

The primary concern of the work book should be the development of your inner life. It is a good idea to write down any dreams or fantasies you have about yourself, to draw or sketch any symbols that evoke feelings in you, whether or not you understand them. The work book is an important document because it is your way of keeping in touch with your inner process.

There are many rea-sons for keeping such a work book, but the most important is to learn to formulate your inner realities for the benefit of your conscious mind. The clearer and more precisely you describe your process, the

ABOVE KEEP A NOTE BOOK TO WRITE DOWN ANY THOUGHTS YOU HAVE ABOUT YOUR TAROT READINGS. THIS PROCESS WILL HELP YOU TO DEVELOP AN AWARENESS OF YOUR INNER SELF.

more satisfied you will be with your progress. While writing, you will need constantly to go back to the cards to see what they actually show or mean. You tend to remember what you want to, not what is there. You will see the ambiguities in your descriptions easily, and will learn with each new view to resolve them in a more fluid manner.

When you have difficult times, or harbour aggressive feelings, feelings of sadness or disgust, you can give them full vent by writing about them in the work book. The images that evoke your inner being will be significant to you for the rest of your life, and it is essential to become familiar with their sources

ABOVE DRAW ANY SYMBOLS THAT HAVE PARTICULAR SIGNIFICANCE FOR YOU. WORKING WITH THE IMAGES IN THIS WAY WILL HELP YOU TO DISCOVER THEIR INNER MEANING.

121

and their mechanisms. You will see that certain symbols recur again and again – they must be telling you something important about your deeper self.

The cards you draw are like the people for whom you do readings – they evoke your inner processes and allow them an avenue to the surface so that they can become a familiar part of your whole rather than an episode that pops up when you least expect it. You will see the resonance between your outer life and inner development, and whether the two are in harmony or out of balance. Tarot pictures your attitude to yourself, and using it as a friend and guide will indicate whether your balancing mechanism, the psyche, is being fully used.

Expand your vocabulary of cards until you know them all. Experiment with other decks that explore different symbol systems, such as goddess or astrological tarots or antique decks. The broader your interests in these ideas, the more fully engaged in the world of the psyche you are. Tarot is truly a guide to enlightenment.

GLOSSARY

Aether – The quintessence, the fifth element, an invisible force that unifies the other four elements.

Affirmation – A statement or declaration repeatedly made to oneself as a way of training the will.

Arcana – Secret, mysterious or hidden knowledge.

Archetype – The representation or symbol of an energy principle that has been in existence within the human psyche at all times and in all cultures.

Archetypal world – The domain of the archetypes.

Brotherhood of the Rosy Cross – A mystical order, similar to the Masons, which originated in the 17th century; also called the Rosicrucians.

Cabbala – The mystical teaching of Judaism that has the diagram known as the Tree of Life as one of its central aspects.

Caduceus – A wand with two snakes entwining it, surmounted by wings or a winged helmet, which symbolizes energy, healing force or the integration of lower and higher being.

Cardinal – An astrological term meaning the initiatory or activating principles and houses.

Cartomancy – Telling fortunes with tarot or other cards.

Chakras – Energy centres within the body that govern and modulate physical, mental and spiritual being.

Collective unconscious – A level of consciousness beyond the personal unconscious in which the past common experiences and the acquired wisdom of the human species are stored.

Conscious – The part of our psyche that is concerned with adjustment to external reality.

Disidentification – Consciously releasing one's identification with a particular way of being or subpersonality in order to step outside and observe it.

Divination – The process of arriving at the answer to a question by interpreting symbolic patterns created naturally or by one's own actions, such as with the tarot.

Ego – The vehicle of our own personal goals and objectives in life, which lies at the centre of the field of consciousness.

Esoteric – Inner teaching only available to initiates.

Exoteric – Outer teaching available to everyone.

Fixed – An astrological term signifying sustaining or unchangeable principles or houses.

Gematria – A mystical system of correlations of numbers with the letters of the Hebrew or Greek alphabet.

Golden section proportion – A geometric ratio in which two parts have the same relationship as the larger part to the whole, found in natural growth processes.

Hermetic – A body of mystical literature celebrating the mysteries of the Greek god Hermes.

Individuation – A gradual process of understanding and bringing into balance the different components of the psyche and thereby making the person whole.

Karma – Our attachment to previous patterns of being and action in this and previous lives.

Lemniscate – A closed curve having the form of a figure-of-eight.

Magic – The act of utilizing the will to achieve an end.

Magical weapons – The sword, wand, pentacle and cup are instruments symbolizing the forces of mind, energy, matter and feelings available to the magician.

Mandala – A circular meditation diagram expressing the principle of wholeness.

Mantic art – An art of divination.

Mantra – Spoken or hummed syllables that are the secret seed or essence of a divinity; used in Eastern religious practices to concentrate the mind and join with the godhead.

Meditation – A technique for stilling the mind, for achieving focus or concentration, often using breathing, sounds or images as a basis.

Mutable – An astrological term signifying movable or changeable principles or houses.

Myth – Stories of goddesses, gods, heroines and heroes that illustrate archetypal principles.

Numerology – A system of attributing qualities to the sequence of numbers.

Order of the Golden Dawn – A mystic order founded in the 19th century in which A.E. Waite and Aleister Crowley were initiates.

Planetary spheres – The ancients visualized planetary spheres surrounding Earth, each ring containing gods and goddesses. Ascending through the spheres meant moving from lower lunar unconsciousness to higher levels of godlike being.

Psyche – All psychological processes, both conscious and unconscious, including the soul and mind, the centre of which is the ego.

Psychosynthesis – A system of techniques to evoke and facilitate psychological integration.

Querent – An individual asking a question or consulting the oracle.

Rosicrucian – A Renaissance mystical Order of the Rose Cross founded by Christian Rosencreutz.

Rota – Latin for wheel, and an anagram of taro.

Sephiroth (pl. sephira) – Emanations from the divine that manifest in the four worlds as phases of evolution or consciousness, or steps through which the soul unfolds its realization of the cosmos.

Shadow – Undeveloped or unconscious aspects of our personality that we tend to hide, repress or project onto others.

Subpersonality – One of the many possible components of the total personality, each of which acts in its own way.

Suit – In tarot, the suits pentacles, wands, cups and swords are related to a magical weapon, element or psychological function.

Symbol – A manifestation of an archetypal pattern that carries multiple meanings.

Synchronicity – A connecting principle of events, feelings, or states of mind that goes beyond cause and effect, and functions through meaningful coincidence.

Torah – The Hebrew book of the law.

Transpersonal – The universal core of being that lies beyond the personal realm.

Trumps – derived from the Latin *trionfi*, a circular procession, but now the superior cards.

Unconscious – All thoughts and feelings, both personal and collective, of which we are not conscious.

Western Mystery Tradition – A traditional system of hidden knowledge passed on in the West and originating from Egypt and Greece.

Will – The psychological function that tends to bring the personality in line with the purposes of the higher self.

Yin-yang – A Chinese symbol of spiralling masculine and feminine forces.

FURTHER READING

Anonymous, *Meditations on the Tarot*, Element, Shaftesbury, 1991.
Arrien, Angeles, *The Tarot Handbook*, Aquarian Press, London, 1991.
Assagioli, Roberto, *Psychosynthesis*, Crucible, London, 1990.
Blakeley, John, *The Mystical Tower of the Tarot*, Watkins, London, 1974.
Butler, Bill, *Dictionary of the Tarot*, Schocken Books, New York, 1978.
Campbell, Joseph & Roberts, Richard, *Tarot Revelations*, Vernal Equinox, San Anselmo, 1979.
Camphausen, Rufus, *Mind Mirror and Tree-of-Life Tarot Cards*, privately published, Amsterdam, 1981.
Cavendish, Richard, *The Tarot*, Chancellor Press, London. 1975.
Circiot, J. E., *A Dictionary of Symbols*, Routledge, London, 1988.
Count Goblet d'Alviella, *The Migration of Symbols*, Aquarian Press, Wellingborough, 1979 (1892).
Crowley, Aleister, *The Book of Thoth (Egyptian Tarot)*, Samuel Weiser, York Beach, 1975 (1944).
Ferrucci, Piero, *What We May Be*, Turnstone Press, London, 1982.
Fortune, Dion, *The Mystical Qabalah*, Ernest Benn, London, 1974.
Greene, Liz and Sharman-Burke, Juliet, *The Mythic Tarot*, Rider, London, 1986.
Haich, Elisabeth, *The Wisdom of Tarot*, Allen & Unwin, London, 1985.
Hoeller, Stephen, *The Royal Road*, Quest Books, Wheaton, 1975.
Jacobi, Dr Jolande, *The Psychology of C. C. Jung*, Kegan Paul, London, 1942.
James, Laura DeWitt, *William Blake and the Tree of Life*, Shambhala, Berkeley, 1971.
Jung, Carl C., *Psychological Types*, Kegan Paul Trench Trubner, London, 1923.
Kaplan, Stuart R., *The Classical Tarot*, Aquarian Press, Wellingborough, 1972; *The Encyclopedia of Tarot*, U.S. Games Systems, New York, 1978.
Knight, G., *A Practical Guide to Qabalistic Symbolism*, Vol. Two, Kahn & Averill, London, 1986; *The Treasure House of Images*, Aquarian, Wellingborough, 1986.
Mann, A. T., T*he Mandala Astrological Tarot*, Harper Collins/Thorsens, London, 1987 and 1997.
Nichols, Sallie, *Jung and Tarot*, Weiser, New York, 1980.
Ouspensky, P. D., *A New Model of the Universe*, Kegan Paul, London, 1931.
Smith, Caroline and Astrop, John, *Elemental Tarot*, Dolphin Doubleday, London, 1988.
Tilley, Roger, *Playing Cards*, Weidenfeld and Nicolson, London, 1967.
Waite, Arthur Edward, *The Pictorial Key to the Tarot*, Rider & Company, London, 1974 (1910).
Walker, Barbara G., *The Secrets of the Tarot*, Harper & Row, San Francisco, 1984.
Whitmore, Diana, *Psychosynthesis Counselling in Action*, Sage, London, 1991.
Williams, Charles, *The Greater Trumps*, Sphere, London, 1975 (1932).

INDEX